Ad
Infusing Critica. ⸺⸺⸺⸺ MW01148898

"The ability to think critically is vital to our capacity to 'routinely confront dishonesty' in Linda Nilson's words. In this lively and accessible book, Nilson reviews how students can be helped to investigate claims made across a wide range of disciplines. She provides numerous examples of classroom exercises and assessment formats for college teachers seeking practical guidance on how to infuse critical thinking across the curriculum."—***Stephen Brookfield***, *Distinguished Scholar, Antioch University*

"This book should be read and used by every faculty member. Improved critical thinking is an essential outcome for all courses and for research training in any field. Nilson has drawn on her long experience as an outstanding faculty developer to make it easier for any of us to foster advanced critical thinking. She clearly explains the underlying rationale and provides powerful ways to engage students. She includes (a) a quick and accurate review of major alternative frameworks, (b) extensively developed examples of ways to implement each of them with students, and (c) multiple approaches to assess students' thinking while fostering further sophistication. I would have been a much more effective teacher if I had had this foundation to build on."—***Craig E. Nelson***; *Professor Emeritus, Biology, Indiana University; and Founding President, International Society for the Scholarship of Teaching and Learning*

"Linda Nilson does the seemingly impossible: unpacks the multifaceted, varied definitions and approaches to critical thinking and then deftly weaves them into a rich set of useful approaches and strategies for instructors to integrate into their own outcomes, assignments, and assessments. From making the case for complex thinking in a fractured world, to unpacking the central components of critical thinking across a dizzying array of disciplines, to explicitly nurturing students' dispositions toward high-level thinking, to enhancing existing assignments and assessments, Linda Nilson has created the definitive, inspiring guide to integrating critical thinking into 21st-century instruction."—***Patty Payette***; *Executive Director, Ideas to Action; and Senior Associate Director, Delphi Center for Teaching and Learning, University of Louisville*

"We often say that critical thinking is not only among the key attributes employers seek in college graduates but also an essential quality for informed citizens in a democracy. Yet there's a marked lack of clear guidance for how educators can teach critical thinking in the classroom. Linda Nilson's book performs an essential service by showing faculty how they can teach critical thinking while also teaching disciplinary content, thereby helping students gain an essential skill for life after college, in their professional, personal, and public life."—*Gleb Tsipursky, Author, The Blindspots Between Us: How to Overcome Unconscious Cognitive Bias and Build Better Relationships*

INFUSING CRITICAL THINKING INTO
YOUR COURSE

INFUSING CRITICAL THINKING INTO YOUR COURSE

A Concrete, Practical Approach

Linda B. Nilson

1996–2021 25TH ANNIVERSARY

Sty/us
PUBLISHING, LLC.

STERLING, VIRGINIA

Published by Stylus Publishing, LLC.
22883 Quicksilver Drive
Sterling, Virginia 20166-2019

Library of Congress Cataloging-in-Publication Data
Names: Nilson, Linda Burzotta, author.
Title: Infusing critical thinking into your course : a concrete, practical approach / Linda B. Nilson.
Description: First edition. | Sterling, Virginia : Stylus Publishing, LLC, 2021. | Includes bibliographical references and index. |
Identifiers: LCCN 2021005585 | ISBN 9781642671681 (hardback) | ISBN 9781642671698 (paperback) | ISBN 9781642671704 (library networkable e-edition) | ISBN 9781642671711 (consumer e-edition)
Subjects: LCSH: Critical thinking--Study and teaching (Higher) | College teaching.
Classification: LCC LB2395.35 .N55 2021 | DDC 370.15/2--dc23
LC record available at https://lccn.loc.gov/2021005585

13-digit ISBN: 978-1-64267-168-1 (cloth)
13-digit ISBN: 978-1-64267-169-8 (paperback)
13-digit ISBN: 978-1-64267-170-4 (library networkable e-edition)
13-digit ISBN: 978-1-64267-171-1 (consumer e-edition)

Printed in the United States of America

All first editions printed on acid-free paper
that meets the American National Standards Institute
Z39-48 Standard.

Bulk Purchases

Quantity discounts are available for use in workshops and for staff development.

Call 1-800-232-0223

First Edition, 2021

In memory of my father,
who taught me critical thinking at his knee
and who I miss every day

CONTENTS

PREFACE

I was not intending to write this book. I recall a *60 Minutes* interview with prolific fiction writer David Cornwell, better known by his pen name John le Carré, on September 14, 2017 (Orlando & Silvio, 2017). At the time of the interview, Cornwell had published dozens of novels, including *The Spy Who Came in From the Cold,* and had long passed standard retirement age. Correspondent Steve Kroft asked him why he was writing yet another one. He said something similar to this: "Like an alcoholic, I tell myself that just one more won't hurt." I *so* get it.

Still, this book is needed, it seems. Its objective is to lead you out of the thicket that has grown around the literature on *critical thinking*—a concept that is murky, abstract, overused, and ill-defined to begin with. Not that it has never been defined. Every scholar in the literature has defined it, but there is no clearly agreed-upon definition (Jenkins, 2017; Paris, 2016). It's no wonder polls and surveys reveal that few college-level faculty can define critical thinking or know how to teach it (Paul et al., 2013). Still, critical thinking keeps appearing in Quality Enhancement Plans (QEPs) and professional-program accreditation standards.

The good news is that we do know that critical thinking can be taught (Abrami et al., 2008, 2014; Edwards, 2017; Flaherty, 2017; McConnell & Rhodes, 2017; Schlueter, 2016; Willingham, 2007). But the concept cries for simplification, translation into discipline-relevant course outcomes, tangible teaching strategies, and concrete assessment techniques. I hope to meet these needs in this volume.

Like a course or a workshop, this book proposes learning outcomes for you the reader—promises of what you'll be able to do after reading it. You should be able to

- explain what critical thinking is in simple terms that you and your students can carry around in your heads;
- convincingly explain to your students why it is important for them to learn, in terms of both what they will gain by learning it and, if they tune out, what they stand to lose;
- explain why critical thinking is so challenging to teach;
- overcome the challenges that teaching critical thinking presents;

- identify the type of course content to which critical thinking can be applied and, therefore, that you can use to teach critical thinking;
- integrate critical thinking into the design of a new or existing course in any discipline;
- write assessable critical thinking learning outcomes that are compatible with and make sense in your discipline;
- introduce your students to critical thinking topics by clearing away their misconceptions about it and giving them some grounding in its vocabulary;
- foster in your students the metacognitive and self-regulated learning practices that critical thinking demands;
- foster in your students the character and intellectual traits, virtues, and dispositions that critical thinking requires and promotes;
- ensure that your students observe and articulate their reasoning behind the claims they make—an essential part of critical thinking;
- select and adapt activities and assignments that will give your students no- or low-stakes practice with feedback in critical thinking using a variety of questions, tasks, and teaching methods;
- advance your students' critical thinking skills through your course using one of two strategies of your choice—one strategy offers three structured options;
- compose well-designed objective items—true/false, matching, multiple-choice, and multiple true/false—that can assess most critical thinking skills;
- delimit the critical thinking skills that objective items can and cannot assess;
- design constructed-response questions and tasks that give sufficient guidance and authentically assess critical thinking skills in assignments and tests;
- improve your existing constructed-response prompts by increasing their specificity and raising the level of thinking they require;
- formulate meta-assignments (assignment wrappers) to accompany your students' critical thinking constructed responses so that they can monitor and evaluate their critical thinking processes;
- write two types of high-quality assessment rubrics that focus on critical thinking skills;
- write specifications for critical thinking constructed responses, if you prefer to specs grade (Nilson, 2015) these responses; and
- articulate the possible costs of expressing the conclusions that critical thinking can generate.

The job of a faculty member is not easy these days. You have to make your students feel welcome and safe in your course, create community among them, monitor their mental health, compensate for their lack of preparedness, balance course structure and policies with flexibility, grade a steady flow of assignments and tests, give your students copious feedback on their work, keep tabs on their course progress, keep them apprised of their progress, contact and try to "save" those who are failing to make normal progress, and at the same time convince them to take responsibility for their progress. You have to teach them not only your course content but also how to learn it, how to behave appropriately in the classroom and online, how to read the academic material you assign, how to prepare for tests, how to learn from graded tests and assignments, how to write in your discipline, and how to express themselves without offending others.

Administrative responses to the COVID-19 pandemic have taken shape for the 2020–2021 academic year and beyond, and they entail still more faculty duties: heavier teaching loads for some; the restructuring of courses for increasingly digital platforms; more challenging, policy-changing committee work; additional student advising; more collaboration with other units; and new government lobbying and student recruitment responsibilities—all spread among fewer colleagues and with less funding and administrative assistance. In addition, concerns about job security will worsen for most (Alexander, 2020).

And now add to the lengthy to-do list, teaching students how to think critically. Such wide-ranging and time-consuming responsibilities didn't exist in the academy a few decades ago. As your job has expanded over the years, I have come to see my mission as making your complicated job easier, if just a little easier. This is the goal I set for this book, and I aspire to achieve it with you and for you.

Linda B. Nilson
Anderson, SC
November 2020

ACKNOWLEDGMENTS

When I was in elementary school, my father, who was quite the history buff, took an interest in what I was learning in my classes, especially in history and religion. I told him, and he would then proceed to correct some of the "facts" I was getting. That taught me a lot—that organizations (and the adults within them) lie to others or delude themselves and either way can't be trusted; that an organization's self-interest determines the information it puts out; and more generally, that "it ain't necessarily so." Of course, I got in trouble at school sometimes for expressing any doubts about the material we were being taught, but that just proved my father's points. This was my introduction into critical thinking, and the lesson stuck with me. When "Question Authority" became a mantra for my generation, I thought, "But, of course! Just like Dad told me." This is why I dedicate this book to him. Although it has been several years since his passing (at age 104, incidentally), I miss him every day.

This book wouldn't even exist if it weren't for my editor at Stylus, David Brightman. He approached me about writing it, and my first reaction was, "No, I'm loving my retirement (actually, semiretirement), but I'll give you a chance to talk me into it." And he did. He brought up points like my legacy, the quality of the online critical thinking course I'd designed and recorded for Magna Publications, and the need for the book, which made me give more serious consideration to the idea. I told him I'd start gathering materials together and drafting an outline to see how it felt working on a book again. Somewhat to my surprise, it felt good—really good. Plus, I felt so honored having my favorite publisher ask me to write a book—and on a topic close to my heart. How could I pass on this opportunity? When I let David know that I'd write the book, he was delighted, and I guess I was, too. Thank you, David, for making such a convincing case!

Thanks are also due to several colleagues who, with me, attended the 2019 conference of the Professional and Organizational Development Network in Higher Education and applauded the idea and approach of this book. A special shout-out to Patty Payette, senior associate director of the University of Louisville's Delphi Center and internationally known expert in critical thinking, who shares my impression of the critical thinking literature and really appreciates this book's perspective on it. In addition, Dannelle

Stevens, professor of curriculum and instruction in the Graduate School of Education at Portland State University, graciously helped by providing some key references on writing and thinking.

Over the years I have given a number of faculty workshops and keynotes on teaching critical thinking at various institutions—Clemson University on an annual basis for several years, San Jacinto College in Pasadena, Texas; Meharry Medical College in Nashville, Tennessee; the University of South Florida; the University of Mississippi; the University of Cincinnati; Colorado Mesa University; the University of New England; Simmons University in Boston, Massachusetts; the University of La Verne in La Verne, California; Greenville Technical College in Greenville, South Carolina; and at two SACSCOC Institutes on Quality Enhancement and Accreditation, the Southern Regional Honors Council meeting in Nashville, Tennessee, and a Teaching Professor conference. Some of the colleges and universities had selected critical thinking for their Quality Enhancement Plan. In addition, I recorded online seminars and a course of eight units of presentations on critical thinking for Magna Publications. The course included required readings, homework worksheets, discussion/thought questions, multiple-choice checks-on-learning, and additional resources. Thanks are due to all the faculty who provided me with feedback that helped me make my presentations and, therefore, this book more useful, concrete, and effective.

My husband Greg Bauernfeind never hesitated to lend his support to this project, even though he knew from experience how much time he'd be spending alone and how much cooking he'd have to pick up. He thought the book was an excellent idea from the start, and he celebrated my progress with me. Thank you, Sweetheart!

PROMOTING CRITICAL THINKING TO YOUR STUDENTS

Being Nobody's Fool

Today's students, young and older, crave relevance, and they do not assume that what we have to offer them in college qualifies as relevant to their lives. They need convincing that they will be using the knowledge and skills that we teach them in their work or their lives beyond work. Therefore, we have to make the case. We have to make them care about learning these skills. Fortunately, we have the data and countless illustrations from everyday life to make critical thinking relevant to them in most domains of life.

"So You Want a Job?": Skills Employers Want in College Graduates

Arum et al. (2012) wrote a report published by the Social Science Research Council based on the postgraduate progress of more than 900 students from the troubling study, *Academically Adrift: Limited Learning on College Campuses* (Arum & Roksa, 2011; more on this study shortly). The team found that the graduates whose scores on the critical thinking section of the Collegiate Learning Assessment (CLA) fell into the bottom 20% were three times more likely than those who scored in the top 20% to be unemployed (9.6% versus 3.1%). More generally, the former graduates were living a less desirable lifestyle than the latter ones.

Going back at least 15 years, American companies have voiced a need for graduates who can think analytically, communicate clearly, and work well with others. An organizational collaboration including the Partnership for 21st Century Skills surveyed human resource managers about their skill needs (Casner-Lotto & Barrington, 2006). In a list of 30 different skills and content domains, these managers prioritized oral and written communication skills, collaboration skills, professional and work ethics, and critical thinking and problem-solving skills as most important.

The demand for critical thinking skills is still there. An education website for college-educated job seekers called Skills You Need devotes an entire page to critical thinking (Skills You Need, 2019). According to a survey conducted by the National Association of Colleges and Employers in 2018, employers are overwhelmingly looking for the following skills and abilities on résumés: written communication (82% of employers), problem-solving (81%), teamwork (79%), initiative (74%), and analytical/quantitative reasoning (72%) (Doyle, 2019; NACE staff, 2018). In particular, employers want people who can apply analytical skills in interpreting large amounts of data. Analytical skills ranked third in LinkedIn's company survey, right behind the technical skills of cloud computing and artificial intelligence. While collaboration ranked high on a "soft skills" list (Patrone, 2019, para. 7), communication skills and ethics failed to make any list in the LinkedIn survey.

Looking to the future, Kuh (2019) argued that the competencies that students need for the future—that is, for jobs that don't yet exist—include critical thinking and analytical reasoning, along with certain dispositions:

> We've known for many decades that there are no short cuts to cultivating the habits of the mind and heart that, over time, enable people to deepen their learning, develop resilience, transfer information into action, and creatively juggle and evaluate competing ideas and approaches. These are the kinds of proficiencies and dispositions needed to discover alternative responses to challenges presented by the changing nature of today's jobs or for work not yet invented. Workplaces, societal institutions, and the world order are only going to get more complicated and challenging to navigate and manage, increasing the need for people with accumulated wisdom, interpersonal and practical competence, and more than a splash of critical thinking, analytical reasoning, and altruism. (para. 7)

Are employers getting the college graduates that they want? Apparently not in the area of critical and analytical thinking. Recall that human resource managers rated professional and work ethics, oral and written communication, collaboration, and critical thinking and problem-solving skills as the most important criteria in hiring new college graduates. They also said that too many prospects were lacking these skills (Casner-Lotto & Barrington, 2006). According to PayScale's survey of almost 64,000 managers, 60% of the respondents complained that their new hires with bachelor's degrees lacked the critical thinking and problem-solving skills that their jobs required (Strauss, 2016).

In addition to surveys of business and industry managers, scholarly research has also uncovered deficiencies. Osborne (2010) chides college-level science educators for not even trying to develop critical reasoning and argumentation skills in their students. Deficiencies in general were documented in *Academically Adrift*, which caused quite a stir as soon as it came out. Following a respected methodology, Arum and Roksa (2011) conducted a longitudinal national study of involving 2,300 undergraduates at 24 academically representative institutions to find out what cognitive skills students improved in college. Their disturbing headline finding: 36% of students showed no significant gains in critical thinking, complex reasoning, and written communication from freshman year to graduation, and 45% of students showed no gains after 2 years. (Predictably, the gains were greater among students majoring in the arts and sciences than in more practical, job-oriented majors such as business.) We could also argue that 64% of students improved significantly on these skills, but even so, the 4-year effect size was a modest .47. Huber and Kuncel's (2016) meta-analysis of 71 studies on students' critical thinking gains in college paints a somewhat brighter picture, but mainly because of the more sizable gains that were recorded in earlier decades.

Employed graduates have also weighed in on this issue, most recently in a 2019 Elon Poll of 1,575 college graduates, age 18 to 34, living in the United States in 2019. They were asked to select the skills they needed and used on regular basis.

- A majority (59.7%) reported that "researching and understanding the answers to complex questions" was a "very important" skill in their day-to-day work life, and 7.4%, a "somewhat important" skill (Elon University, 2019, p. 6).
- A majority (58.2%) said that "using and/or interpreting data" was a "very important" skill in their day-to-day work life, and 7.7% said that it was a "somewhat important" skill (Elon University, 2019, p. 6).

Researching and understanding answers to complex questions and using and interpreting data fall squarely into the category of critical thinking skills, and roughly two thirds of employed college graduates say that they routinely need one or both of them in their jobs. Commerce and government cannot run without them. These are facts that our students need to know.

Beyond Employment: Quality of Life

Because so many of our students take our courses in order to get a job, a better job, or a promotion, they understandably focus on employment as the measure of course-material relevance. But this measure alone unnecessarily limits the benefits that learning bestows. Critical thinking in particular reaps a wide array of advantages in this modern world, including financial advantages. So perhaps we can persuade our students to embrace critical thinking by speaking to not only their employment anxieties but also their monetary concerns. Without breeding cynicism or nihilism, critical thinking engenders a healthy skepticism and distrust in the promises and rationalizations that come from the political world, institutions, and mass and social media, especially those messages that enter your world without your explicit invitation.

Before we consider the contexts in which we routinely confront dishonesty, let's examine its various versions. It comes in many more subtle and less blatant forms than out-and-out lying:

Vagueness: a vague statement that can't be pinned down as a lie but gives an overall misleading sense.

Glittering generality: an emotional appeal to valued concepts (such as love of country) that distracts from a lack of relevant supporting information.

Willful ignorance: sharing incorrect information by purposefully choosing not to learn or understand the relevant facts.

Lie by omission: deceiving by deliberately omitting relevant information.

Confabulation: making false statements due to incorrect memories, without a deliberate intent to deceive.

Deceptive hyperbole: distorting reality by deliberately exaggerating or minimizing some aspect of it.

Obfuscation: deliberately making the information unclear and confusing without actually lying.

Gaslighting: when confronted by evidence of having lied, attacking the veracity of the truthful source (or purposefully causing someone to doubt their accurate perceptions of reality). (Tsipursky & Ward, 2020, pp. 34–35)

Some individuals and organizations take advantage of human psychology by exploiting the *illusory truth effect*, which is our tendency to believe something we hear or read frequently and repeatedly. More than scholarly studies that appear in the journal *Personality and Social Psychology Review* support its robustness (Tsipursky & Ward, 2020). Closely related is *processing fluency*, which is our increasing degree of comfort with and acceptance of often repeated statements.

Critical thinking can help us detect these more subtle forms of dishonesty and psychological manipulation so that we can rebuff the messages.

Avoiding Scams and Shams

If you Google "scams," you will get almost a half *billion* hits—maybe more by the time you read this. They are online and on the phone. They pertain to merchandise, credit card interest rates, loans, discounts on utilities, banking, tickets to events, travel packages, lotteries, sweepstakes, contests, underpayment to the IRS, charities, fundraising, pyramid and multilevel marketing schemes, investments (e.g., penny stocks and microcap stocks, which need not register with the Securities and Exchange Commission [SEC]), business opportunities, foreign currency trades, franchises, government grants—you name it. But they all have one thing in common: taking your money with no return to you, whether through your credit cards, bank accounts, gift cards, wired transactions, face-to-face transactions, or a simple check or money order. Registering on the National Do Not Call Registry does little to curtail scams. Various sites say how to detect scams—promises of something for nothing; promises of a lot of money for sending in a modest amount (called "advance fee" fraud); and errors in spelling, grammar, punctuation, and sentence structure—and how not to respond to them. But scammers become more and more clever all the time and can—actually do—trick large numbers of intelligent people.

Similarly, a sham is a fraud or hoax, something that is not what it claims to be. The only thing separating scams from shams is convention: Shams are usually larger-scale frauds. Recent ones have reeled in well-educated, wealthy people. Remember Bernie Madoff, who stole $20 billion in principal funds in his $65 billion Ponzi scheme (Smith, 2013)? (Forty-five billion dollars were in "paper returns" that did not exist.) He roped in folks who had the discretionary funds to invest thousands and even millions of dollars into his "portfolio," and these people lost every penny just for trusting Madoff's spiel.

Madoff was just one of many. Portrayed by Leonardo DiCaprio in the popular movie *The Wolf of Wall Street* (DiCaprio et al., 2013), Jordan Belfort manipulated the stock market by cold-calling and enticing unsuspecting victims to put their money in certain stocks. Of course, the prices of those stocks would jump, at which time Belfort's company would sell their shares at big profits, leaving the victims to suffer the losses—a sham called "pump and dump" (Investopedia, 2020). The Wolf had to pay a fine of $100 million and spent less than 2 years in prison, which makes one think that maybe crime does pay (Goldman, n.d.).

Unless you were very young in 2001, Enron should ring a loud bell. The company was a Wall Street honey in the 1990s. But under the direction of founder Kenneth Lay, the company hid billions of dollars in debt, misleading the SEC as well as its shareholders. The cover-up couldn't last forever, and the bottom fell out of the stock, quickly dropping like a rock from $90 to less than $1 per share. Its investors lost over $74 billion, making it the biggest financial sham to date—even bigger than Madoff's. With assets of more than $60 billion, Enron's bankruptcy was also the largest corporate bankruptcy in history (Goldman, n.d.).

Just one more, because it's more current. Theranos, a start-up biotech firm, claimed to have developed a new, revolutionary type of blood test, one that could diagnose hundreds of diseases and conditions from just one drop of blood. Or so declared the company's founding CEO Elizabeth Holmes (a Stanford University dropout) and COO Ramesh Balwani (her boyfriend). Many companies and individuals invested, and renowned national leaders such as former U.S. Secretaries of State Henry Kissinger and George Shultz joined Theranos's board of directors. The start-up was valued at $9 billion, and Holmes herself was valued at $5 billion net. But somehow, the tests were never ready. After many missed deadlines, early prospective customers Walgreens and Safeway backed out of their deals with the company, and the big-name directors exited the board. All the blood test claims proved fraudulent. The SEC fined Holmes and Balwani, both of whom now face criminal charges on nine counts of wire fraud and two counts of conspiracy to commit wire fraud. The victims include the firm's numerous investors and hundreds of employees, many of whom quit good jobs with legitimate companies to sign on with Theranos (Ramsey, 2019).

Unfortunately, I could go on and on about scams and shams. According to the Fraud Research Center, Americans lose $40 to $50 billion to fraud every year, and up to 17% of the adult population falls prey annually to too-good-to-be-true financial shams. Because many scammers and shammers are clever, creative, and motivated, few of us are too smart to be victimized (Farrington, 2020).

Students may wonder: Will taking a course or two infused with critical thinking prevent them from being victimized? Perhaps not, but we *can* tell them that practicing critical thinking on a daily basis will make them much less susceptible. In addition, they (and we) can check the website Hoax-Slayer (https://hoax-slayer.net/) which debunks scams, false rumors, phishing schemes, deceptive emails, and hoaxes on the internet.

Questioning Popularized Research Studies

Remember when caffeinated coffee was deemed bad for you? And 3 years later, deemed good for you (Nichols, 2017)? How about when the medical community encouraged postmenopausal women to start hormone replacement therapy (HRT) to prevent heart attacks, dry skin, osteoporosis, and loss of libido? Then, suddenly, researchers halted a longitudinal study on the effects of HRT because it seemed to be *causing* fatal heart attacks in the subjects at a disproportional rate (Pedersen & Ottesen, 2003). And did you hear that multitasking improves the cognitive skills of senior citizens, along with making them feel young and live longer? These "findings" fly in the face of the well-researched *negative* effects of multitasking, including increased stress, more task errors, and reduced learning (Crenshaw, 2008; Junco & Cotton, 2012; Lepp et al., 2014).

What is going on here? What should you believe? Nothing, critical thinking wisdom tells you, until you find out more about the studies. Are they double- or triple-blind? Do the subjects represent the general population, or are they mostly White and middle class and higher? Do the studies control for race and class? In fact, do they control for *every* variable that may reasonably impact the effects under study? Does the research funding come from a source that stands to gain from positive or negative results? The problem with studies of nutritional supplements is that too many of them are funded by the manufacturers. This means that interested people must dig into the details of the studies on their own, because the mass media give only headlines and soundbites. We can be grateful for the web, but only assuming that we know how to separate the biased sites from the scientific ones.

Not that combing published research guarantees finding valid results. *Nature* reports that the number of retractions of published articles by respectable, peer-reviewed scholarly journals jumped by a factor of 10 in the previous decade (Van Noorden, 2011). The reproducibility of research has also emerged as an issue—in some medical fields, among *most* of the scientific articles (Burton, 2019). Critical thinkers do not believe just one report; they wait for others to come out.

Resisting Advertising

Advertising thrives on appeals to emotion (anxiety, envy, guilt, greed), appeals to tradition, the bandwagon fallacy, half-truths, incomplete information, lies with statistics, star-power testimonials, the illusory truth effect, processing fluency, narrative fallacies (persuasion through a heartwarming story), moral licensing (you work hard, so you're entitled to eat this candy bar), and other fallacies and distortions of the truth. What will your friends and relatives think if they can smell anything but flowers and cinnamon throughout your house? What will your peers think if you're wearing last year's fashions and colors? Aren't the windows (bathroom fixtures, appliances, carpets, flooring, wall treatments, bedding, furniture, etc.) in your home dated? Doesn't the association between this beer and these gorgeous horses (or beautiful women, Mexican beach scene, lively party, etc.) make you feel good? Wouldn't you feel happier and freer if you started taking this new medication for whatever (you think) ails you? Wouldn't this liquor ensure you and your friends a better time than what you've been having lately? Wouldn't this vehicle make you feel cooler/safer/younger/more current/more attractive? Wouldn't this makeup help you look and feel more beautiful and sexier? How much do you really love your baby if you don't use these ultra-soft, ultra-absorbent diapers?

Ads sometimes use statistics, too. "You'll have two times more good hair days" if you use such-and-such a hair product. Where did this statistic come from? And what does it mean? Consider the statement that a certain brand of makeup lasts 24 hours. Under what conditions? If a person is just sitting in a chair for 24 hours, this information is useless, if not out-and-out dishonest, because this condition doesn't represent the way people live their days.

Similarly, products claim to be "the best" in their category. For example, "Nothing keeps you drier than X brand" antiperspirant; "X brand is the most rigged truck made." "The best food for your dog . . . X brand." The critical thinker responds, "The 'best' on what criterion? In what study? Who says?"

Incomplete information distorts the truth in another way, and here is an excellent illustration. Perhaps you've seen the ad for a skin product that "magically" eliminates or at least greatly reduces deep as well as fine wrinkles and bags under the eyes in minutes. While this claim is "valid," the information not included is that the effect lasts only for a couple of hours. Typically, social engagements, especially special occasions, last longer.

If the highly flawed arguments that advertisers present didn't convince people to buy products and services, companies wouldn't spend billions of dollars every year on their ads. These arguments work because few people question them. The receiver has to think and ask about the source, the meaning of the claims, the conditions under which they may hold, the durability of the reputed effects, and other validity holes, such as whether the claimed relationship is truly causal or spurious, statistically unlikely, or based on a fallacy. Only a well-practiced critical thinker is likely to pose these questions and, therefore, take the advertising claims with an entire saltshaker. Stripped bare, an ad is simply an announcement that a certain product or service exists; it provides no reliable information about the product's or service's quality or effectiveness.

Guarding Against Propaganda, Brainwashing, Fake News (Disinformation), Demagoguery, and Double-Speak

Let's open this thorny section with definitions, starting with the most general term, *propaganda*, which is biased or misleading information (misinformation or disinformation) that is put forth to systematically promote a certain political viewpoint or favorable perceptions of a political entity. Its intention is the manipulation of popular beliefs, attitudes, or actions. It uses symbolic means such as words, pictures, slogans, music, flags, banners, signs, insignia, coin and postage stamp designs, monuments, and the like. National holidays, pledges of allegiance, national anthems, and primary-school textbooks in history and civics rank among the first forms of propaganda that children experience. Because propaganda thrives on frequent repetition, it takes advantage of the illusory truth effect.

Brainwashing is such an extreme form of manipulation that the term *propaganda* fails to do it justice. It means forcibly pressuring a person to adopt beliefs, values, or ways of thinking that are unrelated or even opposed to that person's original or prior ones. The techniques usually involve physical pain and deprivation. Whether critical thinking can protect against this kind of heavy-handed indoctrination and conditioning is not clear. Some U.S. military who were prisoners of war in Vietnam (the late Senator John McCain, for instance) apparently did resist brainwashing, but we don't know the role that critical thinking played. Strong patriotic emotions may explain this resistance. Therefore, let's leave the topic of brainwashing and home in on fake news, demagoguery, and double-speak, which represent day-to-day forms propaganda that critical thinking *can* neutralize.

In this politically polarized society we now occupy, each side calls the news reported from the other side "fake news," and it's important to remember that what you call "fake" depends on the side you're on. However, critical thinkers recognize that reality is not all a matter of politically charged perceptions. Except to extreme phenomenologists, "facts" actually exist out there; "alternative facts" do not. Certainly, facts may require interpretation, analysis, and contextualizing to make complete sense out of them. For example, jihadists see their actions as waging a holy war against infidels—a good thing in their eyes. Victims in the Western world view their actions as terrorism. But the "facts" in this equation refer to something that happened (e.g., a hotel bombing, some number of fatalities and injured) and to these differing perceptions and labels of what happened.

So, let's say we hear on one biased news channel or another that one of the U.S. cabinet secretaries is suddenly out of a job. Why, we wonder? One channel says the secretary resigned; another claims that the president fired the incumbent for disloyalty; yet another agrees that the secretary was fired but for some other reason. So what is fake and what is real? We personally cannot know because we probably have no way to verify any of the claims made. The same holds for claims made by our government in some conflict with another government. We can ask, "Did China really walk away from negotiations, or not? What does China claim happened, if we can even find out? And even if we can find out, what really happened?" We cannot determine this on our own.

Of course, we can appraise some claims on our own. While the government rarely reports the annual inflation rate anymore, it declares on occasion that it is as low as 2%. Since we all shop for goods and services, we know whether that reported rate succeeds or fails to represent our reality, and lately it has failed. In addition, the government is free to measure inflation with any "representative" goods and services that it chooses.

Critical thinkers maintain a watchful, robust skepticism, believing no definite side of the mass media or social media. Rather, they make the extra effort to check the facts that can be checked. The following sites are as objective and evidence-oriented as any available:

- PolitiFact (n.d.): The Pulitzer Prize–winning source for political facts versus fictions is owned by the Poynter Institute, known for its credible, evidence-based content. The Poynter Institute also runs the International Fact-Checking Network (IFCN), which sets standards for fact-checkers.
- FactCheck (n.d.): This nonpartisan, nonprofit, award-winning resource run by the Annenberg Public Policy Center at the University of Pennsylvania exposes political deceptions and clarifies issues of confusion.
- FlackCheck (n.d.): This "sister" of FactCheck, also run by the Annenberg Public Policy Center at the University of Pennsylvania, focuses on helping people detect fake news (features how-to video) as well as flaws in political ads and arguments.
- OpenSecrets (n.d.): This site is a nonpartisan, nonprofit resource run by the Center for Responsive Politics that tracks money and lobbying as well as their effects on elections and public policy.
- Media Bias/Fact Check (n.d.): A website that detects fake news and interprets and reports the political bias of almost 3,000 media sources on the internet.
- AP Fact Check (n.d.): Associated Press (AP) journalists from around the world report deceptions in the news.

- Snopes (n.d.): Snopes is a long-time, respected evaluator of urban legends, folklore, myths, rumors, and misinformation.
- Truth or Fiction (n.d.): This site corrects political rumors and exposes hoaxes.

What does "objective" mean? It means that the claims of both sides, all sides, are subject to exposure as false. Consider these two items from FactCheck, which appeared one right after the other:

1. August 21, 2019. White House economic adviser Larry Kudlow claimed without evidence that the United States–Mexico–Canada Agreement would add "180,000 new jobs per year" in the United States (Gore, 2019).
2. August 20, 2019. In a July 31 television interview, Democratic presidential candidate Marianne Williamson inaccurately implied there might be a connection between vaccines and higher reported rates of childhood chronic diseases (McDonald, 2019). She is correct that reported rates of chronic conditions in children have increased over the last several decades, but there is no scientific evidence to suggest vaccines are the cause.

Demagoguery is a manipulative political appeal that plays on people's emotions and popular prejudices rather than their rational side. The term typically applies to a person in politics who uses this strategy. Some people with little sense of history may believe that President Donald Trump, who has tried to arouse the fear and disdain of more groups and individuals than has the average modern politician, inspired the term. But in fact, the ancient Greeks invented it to describe some of their own leaders. Since then, the term has been aptly applied to Adolf Hitler, Benito Mussolini, Joseph Stalin, Senator Huey Long, Father Charles Coughlin, Senator Joseph McCarthy, Senator Ted Cruz (when using religious references), Senator Bernie Sanders (when villainizing corporate leaders), Senator Hillary Clinton (when labeling Trump supporters "deplorables" [Chozick, 2016]), and countless other political leaders. Demagoguery crosses party lines, national borders, and millennia. While effective in the political realm, critical thinkers recognize and dismiss it as a fallacious claim.

Double-speak is the deliberate use of euphemisms or obscure language to distort, cover up, or disguise the truth. Critical thinkers stay on the lookout for such language and translate it back into the unvarnished truth. In these examples, the euphemism is the first word or phrase in the pair, and it is no accident that most double-speak terms refer to political, governmental, military, police, and business actions.

- contribution = political gift or bribe
- austerity = cutting public programs and services to reduce government spending
- restructuring (a company) = firing employees
- downsizing = firing employees
- reducing costs = lowering wages/salaries
- negative cash flow = bankrupt or broke
- misconduct = white-collar crimes committed by politicians, business leaders, the military, professionals, and the police
- detained = arrested
- correctional/detention facility = jail or prison
- peace officers = police
- pacify = to put down rioters or protesters with violence
- settlers = people who settle on other people's land
- detainee = prisoner of war
- collateral damage = multiple unintended deaths of innocent people
- friendly fire = accidental killing of military or civilians on one's own side
- ethnic cleansing = genocide
- occupied = invaded and ruled by enemy forces
- servicing the target = bombing
- preemptive strike = unprovoked attack
- neutralizing = killing
- surgical strike = a bomb or missile attack engineered to be accurate
- enhanced interrogation = torture

Distrusting Social Media

It is tragic that most people get their news from social media. Compared to consumers of news from mass media (television, radio, newspapers, and magazines), social media followers are more likely to harbor inaccurate beliefs and opinions about the world and propagate them to those they know. By using hidden algorithms to filter the news that people receive, social media promote silos of political and social opinions and the illusion of a false consensus around controversial issues. Both of these distortions of reality are reinforced by one's confirmation biases, the illusory truth effect, processing fluency, and the *illusion of superiority*, which is our tendency to consider our abilities and traits better than those of others. To make people's thinking still more biased, research has found that although Facebook and Twitter clearly mark their advertisements as "sponsored content," most readers seem to overlook this designation and fail to distinguish genuine news stories from ads and unauthoritative posts (Tsipursky & Ward, 2020).

Making Better Life Decisions

Brookfield (2012b) put it very plainly:

> The whole point of critical thinking is to take informed action . . . action that is based on thought and analysis, which means there is some evidence we take seriously as supporting such an action. . . . In shorthand terms, we think critically not just to survive, but also to live and love well. And a life in which our actions are based on what we feel are accurate understandings of our situations is likely to be experienced as much more satisfying than a life in which our actions are haphazard and arbitrary. (pp. 12–13)

Sharing his own experience, Brookfield claimed that critical thinking saved his life. It made him question the many faulty assumptions he had about himself, his professional status, and manhood in general that were causing his depression, as well as his assumptions about depression itself that were preventing him from getting treatment.

Who among us does not have false assumptions about ourselves? Or our family members? Or our childhood? Or our spiritual or religious beliefs? Or our political views? Or our social attitudes and values? We all have a level of overconfidence in our own thinking. We all fool ourselves with our own fallacies—for instance, projecting our experiences and viewpoints onto others, making negative *ad hominem* judgments about individuals who we believe have wronged us, or sinking down a slippery slope when we fear possible distant consequences. Such faulty thinking usually makes us feel more comfortable and secure. By contrast, critical thinkers routinely question themselves to try to minimize pulling the wool over their own eyes. They prioritize truth over self-assurance.

In fact, the ability to think critically is more strongly associated with general well-being and longevity than IQ, and students need to know this. Critical thinkers tend to experience fewer difficulties than do others in the academic, health, legal, financial, and interpersonal aspects of their life. In Arum et al.'s (2012) study, graduates who scored in the bottom quintile on the CLA's critical thinking section were twice as likely to still be living with parents (35% versus 18%) and considerably more likely to have credit card debt (51% versus 37%). And this makes sense given that critical thinkers seek and act more on evidence than wishful thinking; strive to minimize their cognitive biases; and can better recognize fallacious arguments, scams, fake news, and the like than most people. In addition, because they are more honest with themselves, they more readily admit, correct, learn from, and avoid repeating their mistakes (Butler, 2017). They also sidestep the mental activity of ruminating about personal problems, which clouds rational thinking (Tartakovsky, 2018).

Critical thinking seems to be related to talking to oneself in the third person. This third-person perspective creates emotional distance between oneself and the problem, which fosters viewing a problem from multiple angles. It is associated with acquiring wisdom and intellectual humility and, more so than IQ, predicts emotional well-being and satisfaction with relationships (Grossmann et al., 2019). The third-person perspective is a great tip to share with students.

Conclusion

We should not expect students to know and appreciate the personal benefits of critical thinking. They are not self-evident, and they have more far-reaching effects on a person's life than almost anything else we may teach them. We need to tell students all that is at stake in learning critical thinking. Indeed, their practicing critical thinking in the pursuit of truth should help them lead "the good life" as well as the examined life.

This chapter has described the personal payoffs of critical thinking. However, in crucially important ways, whole societies benefit when their members become critical thinkers, and the final chapter explains how. At the same time, critical thinking and expressing the conclusions that it yields can also have dangerous consequences—certainly if the conclusions interfere with the interests of more powerful entities than oneself. Chapter 12 will address this "other side" of critical thinking.

2

THE CRITICAL THINKING
LITERATURE

A Sticky Thicket

The literature on critical thinking gives no clear, straightforward ideas on what critical thinking is. Unfortunately, it is fragmented into several different frameworks that, like the departments in most institutions, occupy their own silos.

The thicket that characterizes the literature stems less from out-and-out disagreements and more from the fact that the different frameworks rarely acknowledge or cite one another or recognize the overlap among them. Each framework delineates the cognitive skills that this type of thinking involves, which in a sense constitute a definition of critical thinking. But each one cuts up the pie in different ways, leaving readers of the body of literature with a sense of incoherence. It is not surprising then that the literature turns off some instructors. They understandably prefer to avoid it and rely on easy-to-digest models like Bloom and Associates' (1956) taxonomy of cognitive operations—specifically, the higher-order operations of analysis, synthesis, and evaluation.

However, we will venture into this thicket of literature and will be the better for it, because we will be able to develop a hybrid approach that circumvents the silos and incorporates the best of each framework. In fact, the frameworks intersect and overlay in many areas, which frees us to use the most reasonable terminology for the phenomena at issue.

We will start by describing highlights from each of the frameworks, and only highlights. No doubt you will begin to see overlaps emerge. We will not recount all the formal definitions of critical thinking that are out there until chapter 3. Rather, we will consider the skills that each critical thinking framework emphasizes. They best capture the notion of a *working* definition. Willingham (2007) goes so far as to say that there is no specific set of critical thinking skills—certainly not one that exists outside of a discipline, which is the position that this book endorses. Why? Largely because a disciplinary approach makes it easier for you to integrate critical thinking into your course, whatever your subject matter.

William Perry's Theory of Undergraduate Cognitive Development

Technically, the psychologist William Perry (1968) does not qualify as a critical thinking scholar because he never positioned his theory of undergraduate cognitive development within that literature. In fact, when he published it, there was barely a critical thinking literature. Still, it fits the bill. His model implies that critical thinking develops as a learner acquires increasingly valid understandings of the nature of knowledge. It is a developmental process through which an instructor can consciously lead students by replacing their misconceptions with truer representations of knowledge. While some students may generalize these more valid representations of knowledge across disciplines, others may not. Therefore, faculty should not assume that all students will make this leap.

This section describes only Perry's simpler four-stage model as opposed to his detailed nine-stage version.

Students enter a discipline (and, unfortunately, may also leave it) with a major epistemological misconception about it: that it is an accumulation of facts and terms—period. A statement is either a fact or it isn't, either true or false, and scholars have discovered all that you need to know. Perry aptly calls this stage of black-and-white thinking *dualism*, stage 1. Students see their instructors as authoritative imparters of the facts and correct definitions and their job as students as memorizing these facts and definitions. At this level of thinking, morality similarly conforms to absolute standards of good or bad, right or wrong.

So how can you move your students beyond dualism to the next stage? You can show them examples of uncertainties and unknowns in your discipline, helping them to accept the incompleteness of your field (Nelson, 1993, 2000). To illustrate, if you are in the humanities or the arts, share with your students varied examples of respectable interpretations of certain novels, poems, historical documents, or art works. If you are in the sciences, to include the social sciences, provide some examples of conflicting research findings on the same topic, pressing questions in the field, or differing conclusions derived from the same data.

Accepting uncertainties as features of a discipline will help students disavow dualism and progress to stage 2, which is *multiplicity*. Here students believe that the uncertainties represent a temporary state of affairs that will be resolved over time as enough research accumulates. They fail to realize that uncertainty is inherent in the nature of knowledge because knowledge is a human creation, an interpretation of observations made about an otherwise messy, unsystematic universe, and not a tidy structure waiting to be discovered.

To help your students reach this more sophisticated understanding, you might explain how your discipline has evolved through its history—how its methods have changed or how its dominant paradigm has shifted to accommodate new findings (Nelson, 1993, 2000). Perhaps you can share some scientific or historical unknowns that elude ever being resolved. Then your students should be standing at the threshold of stage 3, which Perry calls *relativism*. In its crudest form, students lose their faith in experts as owners of the "truth" because there is no truth, not in the sense of one "true" answer or interpretation. They feel they can believe in whatever makes sense to them. However, they refine their relativism by setting limits around what makes sense to them. Morally speaking, murder may be reprehensible, but cheating on a test is okay because "everyone is doing it." Intellectually, some facts may be acceptable as facts.

Still, students in the relativistic stage encounter difficulties with the inconsistencies and ambiguities that they have created for themselves. They feel paralyzed to make and act on decisions, and they seek reasons to adopt definitive positions. At this point, faculty can step in to explain that their discipline (and all disciplines) has standards for judging competing explanations, theories, and paradigms, some of which prove to have more support than others (Nelson, 1993, 2000). For instance, historians have assembled new evidence that it was not so much a debate over states' rights that set off the Civil War, but rather the economic concerns of plantation owners over the prospect of losing their slaves. In chemistry, the now-defunct phlogiston theory posited that fire derived from the release of the element phlogiston from combustible bodies. This theory predominated for about a century after German chemist and physicist Georg Ernst Stahl proposed it in the early 1700s. But Antoine Lavoisier disproved it when his experiments showed that fire depends on oxygen in the air combining with substances in these bodies. In both these cases, the new evidence created a shift in scholars' commitment from one theory to another.

However, disciplinary groups have different concepts and standards of evidence, as well as different research methods for gathering and assessing evidence. Because students are unlikely to discern these differences on their own, it is best to clarify your discipline's standards and methods explicitly (Nelson, 1993, 2000). For example, historians and social scientists can rarely run experiments the way that psychologists and natural and physical scientists do routinely, and the fields differ about the acceptability of probabilistic findings.

To return to students' unsettling relativism, they can resolve their discomfort by examining competing perspectives for evidence-based support. The process of studying and choosing perspectives ushers them into Perry's stage 4, called *commitment*. At this level, students experience the effects of their choice of positions and may find that some aspects are positive and others negative. But they also come to recognize that personal and intellectual growth comes from taking on a commitment, examining how it fits with the latest evidence and their experience, and making modifications as needed. The objective is to keep an open mind and an exploratory attitude, always seeking more accurate and more comprehensive perspectives. Therefore, all intellectual and moral commitments are tentative and subject to change throughout life (Nelson, 1993, 2000).

At this point, almost all your students will readily embrace your discipline's current paradigms, theories, and explanations. They will realize the stringent tests to which scholars have subjected them and will not have the background or the evidence to counter them. In a few disciplines, students may offer alternative theories that represent their religious beliefs, but this offers you the opportunity to demonstrate the central role of empirical evidence in science.

Perry derived his theory of undergraduate cognitive development by studying a sample of young men in college. What about women? Do they develop cognitively by the same or different stages? Marcia Baxter Magolda (1992) answered the call by conducting a study on female undergraduate students. The four levels of knowing that she discerned—absolute, transitional, independent, and contextual—reflect more relational thinking than the abstract stages that Perry identified. Still, both models are comparable.

We will briefly revisit Perry's stage-based, developmental framework in chapter 7, the section Advancing Students' Critical Thinking Skills Through Your Course. Because he passed away in 1998, Perry never had his own website, but you can find many websites that summarize his theory, such as Macie Hall's (2013), W.S. Moore's (2001), and William J. Rappaport's (2018).

Unlike Perry's, the next five frameworks came about explicitly for teaching and assessing critical thinking. In the limited space in this chapter, I focus mainly on the critical thinking skills they posit and a few other highlights, but subsequent chapters contain more information on them.

Stephen D. Brookfield's Assumption-Based Approach

Brookfield's (2012a, 2012b) framework of critical thinking relies on identifying *assumptions* and checking them for validity and accuracy. However, Brookfield uses the term to broadly encompass just about every kind of statement. He defines three types of assumptions:

- *causal*—explanations of a sequence of events
- *prescriptive*—recommendations or statements of what should be or should happen
- *paradigmatic*—commonsense, taken-for-granted statements

Causal and paradigmatic claims may be backed by a mountain of evidence, but Brookfield still calls them assumptions. Because they are usually accepted as "fact," paradigmatic assumptions are the most difficult to acknowledge and question.

Brookfield also posits five traditions of critical thinking:

1. *Analytic philosophy* incorporates argument analysis, logic, logical fallacies, and types of reasoning, to include inductive, deductive, analogical, and inferential. In fact, philosophers have argued that their discipline is central to both teaching and learning critical thinking (Oljar & Koukal, 2019).
2. *Natural sciences* rely on the hypothetical-deductive method and standard of the falsifiability of propositions and predictions. Of course, this method relies on all the elements of analytic philosophy and is therefore not really distinct.
3. *Pragmatism* assesses theories and beliefs in terms of their practical application to obtain some desirable result.
4. *Psychoanalysis and psychotherapy* promote introspection into the assumptions that inhibit us from realizing our full potential.
5. *Critical theory* looks at critical thinking as perceiving the hidden power dynamics in a situation and society in general. This includes the ideological manipulations underlying all forms of inequality and intergroup conflict.

In regard to critical theory, you may or may not have among your student learning outcomes the ability to articulate a cogent critique of the current political economy. Of course, just about every nation in today's world and every society starting with the Paleolithic chiefdoms offers plenty of systemic flaws to criticize—corruptions, injustices, inequities, inhumane behaviors toward others, and ideologies to cover up, justify, or legitimize these problems. Modern humans did not invent these. However, we are just like our ancestors who couldn't see the cover-ups, justifications, and legitimizations that past elites promulgated in their societies. Brookfield explicitly has in mind the dominant institutions and ideologies of contemporary societies, such as capitalism, democracy, meritocracy, patriarchy, heterosexism, and White supremacy.

As you will see, every other critical thinking framework falls within analytic philosophy and the natural scientific method to at least some extent. Wolcott's approach largely represents pragmatism. None embraces critical theory or the psychoanalysis and psychotherapy traditions.

Brookfield (2012a) has a large section on his website titled Developing Critical Thinkers that contains his workshop materials and the scenarios that he has created and used in teaching critical thinking.

Peter A. Facione and the Delphi Group

Facione's critical thinking framework falls squarely within Brookfield's analytic philosophy and natural sciences traditions. He assembled a large group of philosophers to use the Delphi method to develop this framework—hence, the Delphi Group. In this structured method of communication, a panel of experts individually completes a series of questionnaires, and after each round, members share their responses within the group. The experts refine their concepts, approaches, and theories as they read and apprise what other members have written, allowing a collective wisdom to emerge. Through this process, Facione (2020) and the group identified eight critical thinking skills—interpretation, explanation, analysis, inference, evaluation, deduction, induction, and numeracy—and developed the well-validated California Critical Thinking Skills Test (CCTST), which assesses these skills in everyday scenarios.

The formal definitions of these eight skills are adapted from Insight Assessment (2013a), the framework's website.

1. *Interpretation*: Interpretative skills allow us to determine the precise meaning(s) and significance of a message or signal, whether a gesture, sign, set of data, verbal message, diagram, icon, chart, or graph. Correct interpretation depends on understanding the content of the message, the interpreter, and the interpretation's purpose. It includes clarifying the meaning of something, determining its significance, and categorizing information.

2. *Explanation*: Explanatory reasoning skills enable us to describe the evidence, reasons, methods, assumptions, standards, or rationale behind our

conclusions about what to believe or do. Using these skills, people discover, test, and articulate the reasons for beliefs, events, actions, and decisions.

3. *Analysis*: Analytical reasoning skills involve identifying assumptions, reasons, and claims and examining their role in arguments. These skills allow us to gather information from charts, graphs, diagrams, words, and documents. They also enable us to identify the elements of a situation and determine how those elements interact by attending to patterns and details. Valid interpretations support analysis by revealing the significance of what something means.

4. *Inference*: Inference skills enable us to draw conclusions from reasons and evidence. We practice inference in forming thoughtful suggestions, hypotheses, and the likely consequences of a set of facts or conditions. Of course, inferences based on poor analyses, misinformation, bad data, or biased evaluations can turn out to be false.

5. *Evaluation*: Evaluative reasoning skills enable us to assess the credibility of claims and the sources behind them and, therefore, to appraise the strength or weakness of arguments. They enable us to judge the quality of interpretations, explanations, analyses, inferences, opinions, beliefs, ideas, proposals, and decisions. High-quality evaluation rests on the evidence, data, reasons, methods, criteria, or assumptions behind the claims made and the conclusions reached.

6. *Deduction*: Deductive reasoning moves us directly from the assumed truth of a set of beliefs to a conclusion that must be true if the assumptions are true. Deductive validity is rigorously logical and clear-cut. It leaves no room for uncertainty, unless we alter the meanings of words or the grammar of the language.

7. *Induction*: Inductive reasoning skills allow us to draw probabilistic inferences about what is true based on contexts of uncertainty, such as analogies, data, cases, prior experience, statistical analyses, simulations, hypotheticals, familiar circumstances, or patterns of behavior. Unlike deductive reasoning, it allows for a highly probable conclusion to be mistaken. Even so, it can provide a solid basis for confidence in our conclusions.

8. *Numeracy*: Numeracy skills enable us to use numbers, measures, and mathematical techniques to interpret or evaluate information. It involves solving quantitative reasoning problems or using quantitative reasoning to make judgments. Beyond computing solutions to mathematical equations, numeracy includes understanding how quantitative data are gathered, manipulated, and represented graphically in graphs, charts, tables, and diagrams.

Insight Assessment (2020) includes a great deal of Facione's and the Delphi Group's work on critical thinking, as well as information on the CCTST.

Diane F. Halpern's Cognitive Psychology Approach

Reflecting Brookfield's analytic philosophy and natural sciences traditions, Halpern (2014) forwards the following critical thinking skills:

- *verbal reasoning*, focused on defending against persuasive techniques in everyday language;
- *argument analysis*, which entails identifying unstated assumptions, fallacies, and other weaknesses in arguments;
- *scientific reasoning*, to include hypothesis testing and related facets of the scientific method;
- *statistical reasoning*, involving probability and likelihood; and
- *decision-making and problem-solving.*

Her popular book for students (Halpern, 2014) is a textbook suitable for a stand-alone course in critical thinking, but it is perhaps best seen as a textbook for a course in cognitive psychology and perception, which is Halpern's scholarly area. She focuses on the typically unconscious, everyday mental operations that distort reality and thought: confirmation bias, false memories, interference, selective attention and perception, change blindness, wishful thinking, heuristics (availability, recognition, and representativeness), cognitive dissonance, susceptibility to a variety of fallacies, and others. Her five critical thinking skills serve as antidotes to these all-too-common mental operations, and she explains these skills clearly using many examples in her book.

The Late Richard Paul and Linda Elder's Foundation for Critical Thinking

Founding leaders of the Foundation for Critical Thinking, Paul, a philosopher, and Elder, an educational psychologist, developed perhaps the most abstract but most well-structured framework of critical thinking (Elder & Paul, 2007; Paul & Elder, 2014). They propose 10 "universal intellectual standards" (Elder & Paul, 2007, pp. 8–9) for evaluating reasoning around a problem, issue, or situation: *clarity, accuracy, precision, relevance, significance, completeness* (or *sufficiency*), *depth, breadth, logic,* and *fairness.* These standards reflect the analytic philosophy tradition and, to a lesser extent, the scientific reasoning tradition. Elder and Paul (2007) mean these standards to be applied to evaluate eight "elements of thought" (p. 5): purposes, questions, points of view, information, inferences, concepts, implications, and assumptions. Using the universal intellectual standards to identify the elements in any problem, issue, or situation should help cultivate eight intellectual traits: *intellectual humility, intellectual autonomy, intellectual integrity, intellectual courage, intellectual perseverance, confidence in reason, intellectual curiosity* (replaced by *intellectual empathy* in Paul & Elder [2014, p. 14]), and *fair-mindedness* (Paul & Elder, 2014, pp. 13–15). We will define and revisit these traits in chapters 3 and 5 of this volume.

Elder and Paul (2010) also offer a developmental model of six progressive stages of critical thinking maturity. We will see the utility of this and other development models when we turn to methods for teaching critical thinking in chapter 7. More than anything, Elder and Paul's model highlights the development of metacognition—that is, one's awareness of one's thinking.

- *Stage 1: Unreflective thinkers* do not perceive the determining role of thinking in their lives and, concomitantly, the connection between their thinking errors and their life problems. Whatever cognitive skills they have developed, self-monitoring and self-assessment are not among them.
  Advice for instructors: Few students reflect on their own thinking, so they don't understand how to evaluate, improve, and overcome problems in their thinking. Your first step as an instructor is to help them become aware of and monitor their thinking.
- *Stage 2: Challenged thinkers* have a nascent awareness of the role that thinking plays in their lives and the link between the flaws in their thinking and the problems in their lives, even if they cannot identify these flaws. At some level, they see that good thinking demands deliberate metacognition.
  Advice for instructors: The next step is to familiarize students with the thinking process—to model your own thinking by thinking aloud, to lead discussions about thinking, to incorporate activities and assignments that require students to monitor their thinking, to help them identify the differences between faulty and sound thinking so they can evaluate their thinking, and to help them see their own ignorance and acquire intellectual humility.
- *Stage 3: Beginning thinkers* recognize that their faulty thinking creates problems in many realms of their lives and that they need to take command of and improve their thinking. However, at this stage,

their realization and their plan for improvement are superficial and unsystematic.

Advice for instructors: When students become aware of flaws in their thinking, they can acknowledge that they can improve it by regularly practicing sound thinking. As with sports, the arts, or any other skill, they need to form good thinking habits, and we can show them what these habits are in view of how the mind works. Good thinking habits include reading for deep comprehension, listening actively, writing clearly, and studying effectively and efficiently.

- *Stage 4: Practicing thinkers* recognize that they need to develop new thinking habits to overcome the pitfalls in their thinking patterns. They now analyze their thinking at the surface but not the deeper levels.

Advice for instructors: Students are now ready to learn that reason requires structures of thought: a purpose to thinking, questions to drive thinking, information to interpret, concepts to clarify interpretations, inferences to make in order to obtain informed answers, assumptions behind their inferences, implications of those inferences, and point of view. When trying to figure something out, instructors should encourage students to routinely consider purposes, questions, information, concepts, inferences, assumptions, implications, and point of view. Then students start to connect these to the subject matter: purposes, questions, concepts, and point of view in history and literature; purposes and problems in math and the sciences; then assumptions and implications. They should also monitor their tendency to think egocentrically and sociocentrically because many of their problems in life stem from their inability to understand the points of view of others.

- *Stage 5: Advanced thinkers* analyze their thinking across their life domains and at deep levels, but not consistently. Because they realize how their mental flaws generate problems in their lives, they acknowledge and try to counter their egocentrism and aim to be fair-minded most of the time.

Advice for instructors: Even though few of our students will ever become advanced thinkers, they benefit by understanding the thought processes of the advanced thinker and working toward that level. Through the discussion method, instructors can encourage them to avoid egocentrism and sociocentrism and to cultivate intellectual perseverance, intellectual integrity, intellectual empathy, intellectual courage, and fair-mindedness.

- *Stage 6: Accomplished thinkers* routinely monitor, evaluate, and strive to improve their thinking in all realms of life. For the most part, they have taken control over their egocentrism and have attained a high degree of fair-mindedness. Critical thinking has become a conscious and intuitive habit.

Advice for instructors: Reaching this level is comparable to becoming a professional pianist, writer, or football player. Still, students gain from knowing what it is and aiming to become one.

The Critical Thinking Community (n.d.) is a good resource for more on Paul and Elder's perspective. Their websites (http://www.criticalthinking.org/ and https://community.criticalthinking.org/) present a rich collection of resources, some free and some accessible for a community membership fee, on teaching critical thinking skills at all educational levels. They offer special resources for teaching engineering students critical thinking. In chapter 7, we will touch on their developmental framework again when we address advancing our students' critical thinking skills.

Susan L. Wolcott's Steps for Better Thinking

Wolcott (2006) and her colleague, the late Cindy Lynch, created a step-based, developmental model for helping students become "better" and ultimately critical thinkers. Their framework has five "performance patterns" (para. 1) from step 0 to step 4, reflecting increasingly effective analysis, problem-solving, and decision-making. An instructor can guide students up the ladder as far as they can go.

This model has a less philosophical, more practical bent than the other ones we have considered because Wolcott is an accounting professor and Lynch was a developmental psychology professor. While containing elements of analytic philosophy and the natural scientific method, the approach mostly reflects pragmatism. From now on, I will refer only to Wolcott.

Step 0, where most students are when they start college, is the *confused fact-finder.* Because they believe that every problem or question has one correct answer, this performance pattern resembles Perry's dualistic stage. According to students at this step, a discipline is composed of facts and definitions that an expert has mastered, and good teaching is simply sharing them.

As the instructor, you can move your students up to step 1, called the *biased jumper,* by asking questions or assigning tasks that prompt them to identify problems, determine and find the relevant information to solve them, and identify the uncertainties and risks associated with different solution approaches. Recall that Nelson (1993, 2000) recommended familiarizing students with uncertainties in the discipline to advance students from Perry's dualism to multiplicity. The important lesson for students is to realize that problems do not have not just one "right" solution but multiple facets and interpretations, each of which requires evidence to assess its appropriateness relative to other options. Still, students misconstrue their charge as choosing one solution and gathering as much evidence as they can to support it.

Obviously, students need to move along to a more sophisticated thinking pattern, the next of which is step 2, the *perpetual analyzer*. To arrive there, students should be willing and able to present evidence-based arguments for varying interpretations, viewpoints, and solutions—that is, take an open-minded approach to the problem or issue. This means that you as the instructor have the role of helping them see and analyze their own biases and limited points of view and then pushing them to explore alternatives. You might ask them questions that induce them to seek and investigate multiple interpretations and positions.

Unfortunately, students may overstretch their detachment and objectivity to the point of not knowing how to choose among the options. If they must choose, on what basis should they decide? Like students in Perry's relativistic stage, they may feel paralyzed to act and will instead "perpetually analyze," as Wolcott puts it.

To progress, these students need guidance in judging the relative merits of their options. Even if all the options have some evidence to back them up, they do not have equal value. As the instructor, you can help your students identify criteria for appraising and prioritizing the various interpretations, viewpoints, and solutions. Of course, evidence needs consideration, but other criteria such as feasibility, cost, esthetics, and cultural standards may also deserve attention. Given reasoned criteria, how do the options compare and rank? What are good justifications for one's conclusions? Once your students can conduct such an analysis and evaluation, they have reached step 3, which Wolcott calls the *pragmatic performer* pattern. Leading them to this stage represents a major achievement for you because this is a very mature and constructive thinking pattern.

Still, step 3 is not the final landing because it invites closure on a problem or issue. Every interpretation or solution has its limitations and flaws. Perhaps it shortchanges a priority that proves more important later on. Perhaps new data become available. Perhaps conditions or requirements change. The matter may be settled for today but not for tomorrow. Persons at step 4, the *strategic re-visioner,* keep an emotional distance from their interpretations and solutions and have a plan to monitor the environment for more information and future changes. They have a mind open to revisiting their solutions and answers and possibly finding better ones. This step recalls Perry's final stage of tentative commitment to the best perspective available.

To help your students attain this mindset, you can pose questions about the flaws and limitations of their conclusions, their strategies for monitoring the environment into the future, and the conditions under which they might reexamine their conclusions or even redefine the problem. It is too easy not only for students but also for managers and professionals to become self-satisfied with their solutions and never consider revising them.

Wolcott's comprehensive website (http://www.wolcottlynch.com/) and faculty handbook, which you can access at the site, contain a wide variety of assignments and activities designed to move students up the ladder of performance patterns, along with examples from many disciplines (WolcottLynch, n.d.). In chapter 6 we will review some of her assignment questions (formerly called "task prompts") because having students answer thought-requiring questions is a key strategy for teaching critical thinking. Her step-based, developmental framework will appear again in chapter 7 in the section titled Advancing Students' Critical Thinking Skills Through Your Course.

Conclusion

How can we make sense of these competing frameworks? In chapter 3, we will get beyond differences in terminology and start identifying points of overlap among them. At the same time, we will consider why teaching critical thinking presents so many challenges.

3

TEN REASONS WHY TEACHING CRITICAL THINKING IS SO CHALLENGING

One reason why teaching critical thinking can be mystifying is the literature we reviewed in the previous chapter. It gives no clear, agreed-upon advice, and general faculty development in instructional skills does not provide sufficient direction. Yet we know that instructors can learn how to teach critical thinking. Those who receive training specifically in teaching critical thinking improve their students' skills more than faculty who do not (Abrami et al., 2008, 2014; Edwards, 2017; Flaherty, 2017; McConnell & Rhodes, 2017; Schlueter, 2016; Willingham, 2007). The frameworks summarized in chapter 2 share some common ground, especially on the challenges that teaching critical thinking presents. The rest of this chapter addresses the overlaps among these frameworks as well as the challenges.

1. Critical Thinking Involves Certain Kinds of Thinking

Let's now array the various definitions of *critical thinking*—and they *do* vary quite a bit.

According to Brookfield (2012a), critical thinking involves three interrelated phases:

1. Discovering the assumptions that guide our decisions, actions, and choices
2. Checking the accuracy of these assumptions by exploring as many different perspectives, viewpoints, and sources as possible
3. Taking informed decisions that are based on these researched assumptions. (p. 14)

28

But when he writes about the "purposes of critical thinking" (p. 6), he offers alternative views based on each of the five perspectives he posits. Here he sees critical thinking as reasoning and analyzing to accomplish certain goals:

From a critical theory perspective: challenge the dominant ideology; uncover power; and counter hegemony.

From a psychoanalytic and psychotherapeutic perspective: understand how behaviors and emotions assimilated uncritically in childhood inhibit the chance to develop their full potential in adulthood.

From an analytic philosophy perspective: understand how arguments are constructed; distinguish between reliable valid evidence and unreliable, invalid evidence; learn to recognize logical fallacies; separate bias and opinion from fact-based argument; identify different forms of reasoning—inductive, deductive, inferential, analogical.

From a pragmatist perspective: constantly review practice situations to research and improve how we can better deal with them consistently; experiment with different responses to difficult problems, being creatively open to new and innovative solutions.

From a natural science perspective: generate, test, and refute hypotheses through controlled experimentation; apply the principle of falsifiability [so something can possibly be disproved]. (pp. 6–7)

Facione's (2020) definition of *critical thinking* sounds quite different: "purposeful, reflective judgment which manifests itself in reasoned consideration of evidence, context, methods, standards, and conceptualizations in deciding what to believe or what to do" (p. 23). Halpern's definition (2014) has a more goal-driven flavor and seems to reflect Brookfield's (2012a, 2012b) pragmatism, even if the rest of her model does not:

The use of those cognitive skills that increase the probability of a desired outcome . . . thinking that is purposeful, reasoned, and goal-directed—the kind of thinking involved in solving problems, formulating inferences, calculating likelihoods, and making decisions, when the thinker is using skills that are thoughtful and effective for the particular contents and type of thinking task. (p. 8)

A close reading of the Foundation for Critical Thinking's website will reveal several definitions of critical thinking of varying lengths. Therefore, let's turn to Paul and Elder's (2014) work in print for this concise definition:

"Critical thinking is the art of analyzing and evaluating thinking with a view to improving it. . . . [It is] self-directed, self-disciplined, self-monitored, and self-corrective thinking." (p. 2) This definition recalls the meaning of metacognition.

Wolcott (2006) dodges giving a definition, perhaps wisely so, by quoting nine widely varying definitions from various academic sources (including an early one from Richard Paul). If she were to define *critical thinking*, she would probably focus on intelligent problem-solving and sound decision-making.

While Willingham (2007, 2019) has published only a couple of articles on critical thinking and does not rank among the major critical thinking scholars, he has contributed a layperson's definition and a cognitive scientist's definition that are worth considering:

> In layperson's terms, critical thinking consists of seeing both sides of an issue, being open to new evidence that disconfirms your ideas, reasoning dispassionately, demanding that claims be backed by evidence, deducing and inferring conclusions from available facts, solving problems, and so forth. Then too, there are specific types of critical thinking that are charac-teristic of different subject matter: . . . "thinking like a scientist" or "think-ing like a historian." (Willingham, 2007, p. 8)
>
> From the cognitive scientist's point of view, the mental activities that are typically called critical thinking are actually a subset of three types of thinking: reasoning, making judgments and decisions, and problem-solving. . . . *Critical* reasoning, decision-making, and problem-solving . . . have three key features: effectiveness, novelty, and self-direction. (Willingham, 2007, p. 11)

While traipsing through this thicket, we have come upon a few terms that keep reappearing: *reasoned/reasoning* (thinking logically), *analyzing, judging/ evaluating, making decisions,* and *problem-solving,* the last two of which imply Halpern's "desired outcome" and Wolcott's objective. The kind of reasoning and logic meant in these definitions seems to be the analytical type, which can be recast as analyzing. Decision-making and problem-solving are both applications of analysis and evaluation. However, one cognitive operation gets short shrift in all these definitions of critical thinking, and that is inter-pretation. Interpretation requires analysis, as when one is interpreting a work of art or a set of observations, but analysis may or may not require interpreta-tion. An argument could be made that interpretation and analysis overlap as types of thinking.

At this point, we can move from the thicket into a clearing by enter-taining a simple, synthetic definition of critical thinking as *interpretation, analysis,* and *evaluation* leading to a *decision* or *problem solution.* A decision or problem solution may be as simple as a sound answer to a question. We can call this a "pocket definition" of critical thinking that incorporates key elements of all the major definitions. Not to ignore Paul and Elder's emphasis on metacognition and improvement of one's thinking, but we will subsume this under topics addressed later in this chapter.

As handy a definition as we have developed, interpretation, analysis, and evaluation are high-level cognitive operations that many students have trouble mastering. Students may not know what the words mean or what the operations involve. They may have never interpreted, analyzed, or systematically evaluated anything before. At the lowest thinking level—that is, dualism, the unreflective thinker, or the confused fact-finder—these operations don't make sense.

Why is synthesis missing from the pocket definition? While a higher-level cognitive operation, Anderson and Krathwohl (2000) sharpened Bloom & Associates' (1956) concept in the direction of creativity, which all critical thinking scholars would agree is distinct from critical thinking.

2. Critical Thinking Requires Intentional, Explicit Infusion Into a Course

Students don't "pick up" critical thinking skills the way they might acquire technical vocabulary or procedures through repetition. The scholars generally agree that students won't learn critical thinking unless an instructor integrates it into a course intentionally and explicitly (Abrami et al., 2008; Burbach et al., 2004; Edwards, 2017; Paul, 2004; Paul et al., 2013). This means that faculty should use the term in the course learning outcomes, the instruction and practice of the skills, and the assessments. Otherwise students might undervalue the skills as mere disciplinary exercises. Burbach et al. (2004) even recommended that critical thinking be the main focus of the course in order to ensure success.

To infuse critical thinking into a course, faculty need to know how to implement essential course design principles—starting with clear, assessable critical thinking learning outcomes and followed by the alignment of teaching methods and assessments with these outcomes. On formulating good outcomes and designing a course around them, readers can consult any of the many books and websites on the topic (Anderson & Krathwohl, 2000; Fink, 2013; Nilson, 2016b; Wiggins & McTighe, 2005). Formulating critical thinking outcomes that make sense in a disciplinary course will receive thorough treatment in chapter 4 of this volume.

3. Critical Thinking Requires Subject Matter of a Certain Kind

The critical thinking frameworks generally concur, if just implicitly through their examples, that critical thinking requires knowledge of some discipline-based subject matter and is best taught within a disciplinary course. Other scholars agree as well (Bonwell, 2012; Schlueter, 2016; Willingham, 2007, 2019). However, Halpern (2014) wrote her book *Thought and Knowledge* to accompany a stand-alone critical thinking course. The book is in itself a course in cognitive psychology, specifically about the unconscious psychological processes that thwart clear and critical thinking.

However, not all content qualifies for critical thinking. The subject matter must demand higher-level thinking and learning rather than memorization, recognition, or simple (noninterpretive) comprehension. Following "cookbook" directions or "plug-and-chug" procedures requires only the ability to read and act on instructions, or to copy-and-paste, or to copycat somebody else, whether solving simple math problems or inserting an IV into a patient. Learning to recite the multiplication tables or to translate a foreign language at a basic level entails no more than memorization.

Other types of content that don't allow for critical thinking include undisputed definitions, conventions, or facts. Here are just a few examples of terms with definitions that are undisputed in their respective disciplines: *force, mass, ionic bonding, intracellular, tax liability*, and *norm*. Contrast these with disputed ones, such as *life, poetry, reality, human capital, disease*, and *abnormal*. Some conventions inspire no debate: the names of the days of the week, the meanings of international street signs, and the periodic table of the elements. Many "facts" are uncontested because of valid and reliable records or a large number of observations: that the planets in our solar system revolve around the sun; that tigers eat meat; and that Samuel Beckett wrote *Waiting for Godot*. In contrast, some phenomena or observations fail to qualify as undisputed facts, such as the cosmological constant, the nature of near-death experiences, the existence of extrasensory perception, and the reality of alien visitations from other parts of the universe.

For critical thinking, a course must have content containing *claims*—that is, statements that may or may not be complete, valid, or the most viable. To unpack this sentence, let's define what a *claim* is, and it can be any of many things: a disputed definition or fact (mentioned previously), a definition of a problem, a belief, a value, an interpretation, an assumption, an explanation, a hypothesis, a prediction, a theory, a solution, an analysis, an argument, a justification, a judgment, an evaluation, a critique, a generalization, an inference, an implication, a contention, an opinion, a viewpoint, a position, a decision, or a conclusion. Whatever form it takes, a claim is for some reason disputed, debated, controversial, suspect, or uncertain.

For what kind of reason? There may be other perfectly respectable competing claims. The evidence supporting the claim may be weak or ambiguous. The methodology behind its support may be new, untested, or controversial. The issue or concept may be ill-defined. The data may be suspect. Or the source of the claim may have a conflict of interest or a lack of legitimacy.

To return to our pocket definition, critical thinking entails an interpretation, analysis, and/or evaluation about a claim.

What claims do your courses examine? Introductory courses that focus only on undisputed definitions and facts may contain no claims at all, in which case critical thinking cannot be taught in them. If this is true of one of your courses, you might take another look at the content to see if you can add some claims suitable for critical thinking. Look to areas of uncertainties and unknowns in your field.

4. Critical Thinking Is Difficult and Unnatural

Critical thinking is a genuine challenge for students and takes time and effort to learn it. As mentioned previously, they may not understand what interpretation, analysis, and evaluation involve. The K–12 school system that socialized them, as well as some college courses, demands only lower-level thinking and rewards compliant behavior, not a critical perspective (Paris, 2016).

To increase the challenge even more, critical thinking compels students to examine their own beliefs, values, opinions, explanations, generalizations, and inferences—all the claims they have held dear—in a diagnostic way. People resist questioning, critiquing, and possibly replacing their mental habits and mental models of how the world works; it's unnatural. In psychology, this tendency to resist is called *confirmation bias*. People want to validate their views of reality so strongly that they selectively seek, perceive, and remember information that will do so (Halpern, 2014; van Gelder, 2005). Critical thinking scholars concur on this point. In fact, van Gelder (2005) contends that learning critical thinking is as difficult as becoming fluent in a second language.

Why are people this way? Both humans and many (perhaps most or even all) animals are wired to recognize patterns and derive general rules about reality from those patterns. Rules simplify a complex and sometimes threatening environment. They make it more predictable, granting a creature some sense of control, reducing stress and fear, and increasing survival chances. Only the failure of one's rules gives reason to doubt and abandon them, assuming one survives the failure. The claims that we endorse constitute our rules, and our identities revolve around them. They are important and dear to us. Therefore, challenging them can generate severe discomfort, which takes time and effort to get passed.

Learning entails struggles. As an instructor, you can help your students surmount these struggles and facilitate their willingness to challenge their mindset and explore alternative ways of thinking. Give them prompt, honest feedback. Help them see how their rules of reality have failed them—perhaps caused them to make unwise decisions; to come to conclusions that later proved costly; or to fall prey to scams, shams, advertising, faulty research reports, propaganda, fake news, and the other deceptions that chapter 1 outlines. In addition, according to research studies, you can help by simply creating a good rapport with your students and communicating your high expectations of them while they are grappling with challenges (Baxter & Bowers, 1985; Murphy et al., 1999; Rosenthal & Jacobson, 1968; Wang & Lin, 2014).

5. Students Bring Biases and Misconceptions That Interfere With Critical Thinking Into Their Courses

Your students probably come to you with beliefs, values, biases, and misconceptions that may obstruct their reasoning about some of the issues your course addresses. Among these biases are egocentrism, which is basing beliefs solely on one's own personal experience, and sociocentrism, which is basing beliefs on what one's society and culture have taught one to believe (Elder & Paul, 2010; Paul & Elder, 2014; Payette & Barnes, 2017). Your students are probably not aware that they even harbor these biases. To help them see beyond their experiential and cultural blindness, Kraus et al. (2013) recommend these reflective prompts:

- What have I been told to believe?
- What evidence supports these beliefs?
- In what other ways can I interpret the evidence?
- How can I fairly evaluate the evidence and alternative interpretations? What additional evidence would help me?
- What are the most reasonable or most likely conclusions that I can draw?

The following questions can also comprise a reflective writing assignment to sensitize your students to their emotional attachments to certain beliefs and values:

- What part of the learning experience is challenging your thinking about the subject?
- Do you find yourself resisting it?
- If so, how can you overcome your resistance?
- Can you simply suspend judgment for a while and try out some new ideas?

Now it is your turn to reflect on your courses:

- What content in courses that is amenable to critical thinking may challenge your students' beliefs, values, biases, and misconceptions?
- What reflective writing task can you assign to your students to help them identify and overcome these barriers to reason?

Your students may also bring to your courses various misconceptions about the nature of critical thinking. They may believe that it is purely negative and critical, or paralyzing (Brookfield, 2012b), or anti-the-way-things-are. Even as they acquire the skills, they may become cynical "self-satisfied debunkers" (Roth, 2010, para. 4) who relish undermining everything that people hold dear. If this happens, they will have difficulty finding or creating meaning in their studies and their lives in general (Roth, 2010). Critical thinking need not lead to this dead end, and it won't if you clear out these misconceptions at the beginning of your course and help your students see and embrace its benefits.

6. Critical Thinking Requires Self-Regulation

Specifically, critical thinking requires metacognition and meta-emotional insight and control. Both of these are dimensions of self-regulation involving the routine practice of monitoring, evaluating, and correcting one's thinking and emotional responses. Brookfield (2012b), Elder and Paul (2010), Facione (2020) and Halpern (1999, 2014) all maintain that critical thinking cannot take place without metacognition or self-regulation. In fact, Elder and Paul's (2010) developmental model of the stages of critical thinking maturity revolves around metacognition. Students should be able to describe and assess their reasoning process as they gather, analyze, and evaluate the evidence on their way to a certain viewpoint or conclusion. They should also be able to explain how they generated multiple approaches or viewpoints, why they eliminated certain ones, and how they decided one to be the best, at least for now. Then they can describe and transfer critical thinking skills to new issues and situations, including one's own life.

Brookfield (2012b) proposes a reflective audit exercise to encourage metacognition after a couple of his critical thinking class activities. After a debate, for example, students should write about how it clarified or confirmed assumptions they held, how it challenged or changed their assumptions, how they reacted to new assumptions or perspectives that emerged, and how they could reality-test those new assumptions. In another of his exercises, students bring two quotes from an assigned reading to class, react to and discuss them in small groups, and then write reflections on several topics, including why they chose those quotes, whether they would choose the same ones again, which quotes they chose to discuss as a group and why, what new perspectives they learned, and what insights they gained about their own thinking patterns and their preferred types of evidence.

Facione (2020) considers *self-regulation* a core critical thinking skill. He defines it as self-consciously monitoring one's thinking in order to question, validate, or correct one's reasoning or conclusions. He offers a series of self-regulation questions focusing on self-evaluation that students should ask themselves at the end of a critical thinking task: How can we sharpen our position on this issue? How appropriate was our methodology, and how closely did we follow it? How solid is our evidence? How can we reconcile any conflicting findings or conclusions? Are we missing anything in our analysis? What should we revisit?

According to Halpern (1999, 2014), a critical thinker must bring certain dispositions to tasks: to commit to putting persistent effort into complex tasks; to resist impulsive urges (e.g., procrastination, jumping to conclusions) and consciously plan and proceed through a line of thinking; to admit error when necessary and exchange current thinking strategies for better ones; and to remain open-minded and flexible. All these dispositions qualify as traits of self-regulated learners and could just as easily come out of a book on self-regulated learning (and have, using different words, in Nilson, 2013).

The evidence that self-regulation enhances students' learning and retention of knowledge and skills is overwhelming, and the list of self-regulated learning activities and assignments that teach students self-regulation is long and varied (Nilson, 2013). Readings, videos, podcasts, lectures (live, recorded, or teleconferenced), problem sets, papers, projects, test preparation sessions, and graded exams all provide occasions for reflection and other self-regulated learning exercises, and you can select prompts that call for critical thinking. After readings, videos, or podcasts, for instance, you can ask students to reflect on the major points or claims made, possible interpretations of statements, the quality of the evidence given, connections to other course material, or changes in their thinking on the topic.

Because it is so integral to critical thinking, we will revisit self-regulation later in this book. You will find self-regulated learning outcomes near the end of chapter 4, more ways to foster self-regulation in chapter 5, and more self-regulation questions and tasks appropriate for assignments near the end of chapter 9.

7. Critical Thinking Requires the Traits of "Good Character"

When used to describe a person, the term *good character* denotes having virtues such as integrity, determination, morality, and inner strength. Self-regulated learning, character, and critical thinking all overlap in that they share certain dispositions, values, and attitudes. In fact, critical thinking scholars have proposed that certain traits associated with good character and self-regulated learning are essential to critical thinking. These traits supply some of the motivation and abilities to practice critical thinking.

Recall from chapter 2 that Paul and Elder (2014) propose the following intellectual traits:

- *Intellectual humility*—recognizing the limits of one's knowledge and points of view, one's prejudices and biases, and the roots of one's self-deceptions
- *Intellectual autonomy*—thinking for oneself in analyzing and evaluating values, beliefs, interpretations, and suppositions on the basis of evidence and reason
- *Intellectual integrity*—being true to and consistent with one's thinking, applying rigorous standards of evidence and reason to oneself, and acknowledging errors and inconsistencies in one's thinking and actions
- *Intellectual courage*—facing and examining opinions, ideas, or beliefs that one finds abhorrent
- *Intellectual perseverance*—continuing to pursue truths, understanding, insights, and rationality in the face of long-term frustrations, struggles, difficulties, and opposition
- *Intellectual curiosity*—cultivating wide-ranging interests and the desire to learn more about the world; replaced by *intellectual empathy* in Paul and Elder (2014)

- *Intellectual empathy*—understanding the assumptions, reasoning, perceptions, and viewpoints of others by imagining oneself in their situations
- *Fair-mindedness*—analyzing and evaluating all points of view according to the same intellectual standards, regardless of one's own interests or points of view
- *Confidence in reason*—believing that rational thinking will best serve the loftiest interests of oneself and others and promote intellectual autonomy and perseverance

The final trait may seem obvious, but confidence in reason may compete with confidence in other sources of knowledge such as revelation, tradition, and authority, and any of these may override reason in certain circumstances. Most of these eight (or nine) traits exemplify good character.

Facione et al. (2000) posit a list of 12 affective dispositions to critical thinking. Paraphrased, they are as follows:

- broad curiosity
- the motivation to be well-informed
- the motivation to practice critical thinking
- confidence in reasoned inquiry
- trust in one's own ability to reason
- open-mindedness
- flexibility in entertaining alternative opinions, analyses, conclusions, and the like
- appreciation of the viewpoints of others
- fair-mindedness
- truthfulness with oneself about one's biases and related blinders
- good judgment in modifying and deferring opinions
- an openness to change one's opinions when called for

Almost all of these qualities echo Elder and Paul's (2010) intellectual traits and Halpern's (1999, 2014) dispositions. They parallel not only practices of self-regulated learners but also qualities of good character.

In his article, "What 'Learning How to Think' Really Means," what Schwartz (2015) calls "thinking" is what we consider to be critical thinking. He reiterates the point that most critical thinking scholars contend—that sound thinking involves more than a list of cognitive skills; that it encompasses moral qualities, good character, what Schwartz calls "intellectual virtues" (para. 6). Not surprisingly, his virtues overlap a great deal with the intellectual traits proposed by Paul and Elder (2014), the 12 affective dispositions forwarded by Facione et al. (2000), and the four task-related dispositions (self-regulated learning behaviors) posited by Halpern (1999, 2014). Following are Schwartz's virtues:

- *Honesty*—comparable to Paul and Elder's (2014) intellectual integrity, Facione et al.'s (2000) truthfulness with oneself about one's biases and related blinders and an openness to change one's opinions when called for, and Halpern's (1999, 2014) ability to admit error when necessary and exchange current thinking strategies for better ones.
- *Fair-mindedness*—the same word used by Paul and Elder (2014) and Facione et al. (2000)
- *Humility*—which Paul and Elder (2014) call intellectual humility and which overlaps with Facione et al.'s (2000) and Halpern's (1999, 2014) dispositions related to honesty as previously mentioned. Indeed, it takes humility to be honest and have integrity.
- *Perseverance*—much the same as Paul and Elder's (2014) intellectual perseverance and Halpern's (1999, 2014) putting persistent effort into complex tasks and resisting impulsive urges and consciously planning and proceeding through a line of thinking
- *Courage*—again, like Paul and Elder's (2014) intellectual courage; living life with honesty and integrity also takes courage.
- *Good listening*—a term not used by critical thinking scholars, yet an indicator of Paul and Elder's (2014) intellectual curiosity and intellectual empathy; Facione et al.'s (2000) broad curiosity, the motivation to be well-informed, and open-mindedness; and Halpern's (1999, 2014) open-mindedness and flexibility
- *Perspective-taking and empathy*—comparable to Paul and Elder's (2014) intellectual empathy and akin to two of Facione et al.'s (2000) affective dispositions—flexibility in entertaining alternative opinions, analyses, conclusions, and the like and appreciation of the viewpoints of others
- *Wisdom*—again, not in the critical thinking lexicon *per se*, but Facione et al.'s (2000) good judgment in modifying and deferring opinions captures a facet of it; Schwartz (2015) and Schwartz and Sharpe (2011) refer to the practical kind that avoids the damaging extremes of the virtues and resolves conflicts between them (e.g., between empathy and fair-mindedness); all the virtues, traits, and dispositions of critical thinking encapsulate different aspects of wisdom

- *Love of truth*—a précis, indicator, or requisite of many critical thinking qualities: Paul and Elder's (2014) intellectual autonomy (not following the crowd) and confidence in reason; Facione et al.'s (2000) motivation to practice critical thinking, confidence in reasoned inquiry, trust in one's own ability to reason, and openness to change one's opinions when called for; and Halpern's (1999, 2014) putting persistent effort into complex tasks, resisting impulsive urges and consciously planning and proceeding through a line of thinking, and admitting error when necessary. If one doesn't love truth, why would anyone adapt these dispositions and, in particular, demonstrate honesty, humility, perseverance, and courage?

The love of truth, which seems foundational to critical thinking, merits elaboration, as it does not take center stage in today's Western world. Schwartz counterposes it to relativism, which in the extreme respects anyone's truth at any time without sufficient (or any) evidence. It also condemns the viewpoints of experts as elitist. Schwartz presents the widespread, out-of-hand rejection of evolution and global warming as examples of this relativism. But you could add the White supremacist perspective; fears about vaccines causing autism; the mistaken belief that more people are alive today than have died during all of human history; and the myth that Columbus was trying to prove the earth was round, when the vast majority of people knew that just from seeing the horizon. That's not to say that Marx was wrong about false consciousness or that the points of view of the oppressed constitute just one group's "personal" truth. People do wear blinders to perspectives that they haven't experienced in their everyday worlds.

You might be thinking of some, if not all of your students who may not be mature or interested enough to fully understand or develop the necessary dispositions and intellectual traits. Chapter 5 (this volume) suggests several ways that you can help your students acquire good character and the traits and dispositions of critical thinkers.

8. Critical Thinking Requires Mental/Emotional Health

Some years ago I studied the existing critical thinking literature to prepare a keynote and noticed a prerequisite for critical thinking that seemed to be missing: emotional/mental health. Mental health doesn't quite overlap with good character or self-regulation, and yet it affects both. Psychological defense mechanisms deny, repudiate, or misrepresent perceptions of reality. How can people critically interpret, analyze, or evaluate aspects of reality if they distort that reality before they even think about it? So I published an article pointing out how psychological defense mechanisms—*psycho-logical fallacies,* as I called them—such as the ones that follow, interfere with and may avert critical thinking (Nilson, 1997):

- *Denial*—removing from one's awareness one's harmful or negative events, impulses, or behaviors to avoid anxiety
- *Displacement*—transferring one's expression of anger, frustration, or other negative feelings toward someone that one is expected to love, respect, or fear onto a safer target, the classic example of which is releasing the anger you feel toward your supervisor at work on your spouse or pet
- *Externalization*—projecting (see "projection" in this list) one's own limitations or flaws onto others; accusing others of one's own negative behaviors
- *Projection*—attributing one's own unacceptable impulses to others
- *Rationalization*—using an excuse or socially acceptable explanation to justify an action or experience that makes one look bad
- *Regression*—avoiding stress or frustration by feeling and acting like a child
- *Repression*—subconsciously forgetting experiences or events or maintaining irrational beliefs in order to cause psychological pain
- *Resistance*—not allowing repressed experiences or events into one's awareness to avoid anxiety
- *Selective perception and recall*—processing or remembering only certain experiences, usually those that confirm one's beliefs or makes one look favorable, while not perceiving or remembering conflicting experiences
- *Suppression*—like repression, only consciously forgetting experiences
- *Transference*—redirecting one's desires, emotions, and expectations of one person to another person
- *Withdrawal*—refusing to stay in an anxiety-producing situation or activity in order to avoid dealing with it

The items in this list represent just a handful of dozens of psychological defense mechanisms. These mental operations may or may indicate what psychologists and psychiatrists would diagnose as mental or emotional illness because they need not signify a problem. No matter how mentally or emotionally healthy we are, we all occasionally fall prey to one or another of them for at least a period of time. For instance, when we first learn of the death of a loved one, it is normal to initially engage in denial for a short while.

In fact, some of the defense mechanisms can have positive results. For example, suppressing distracting thoughts about an upcoming vacation or current love interest while working can increase a person's productivity and efficiency.

Of a much more serious nature are certain personality disorders—specifically, narcissistic personality disorder, psychopathy, and sociopathy (antisocial personality disorder) (American Psychiatric Association, 2019). While not completely out of touch with reality, people with these mental illnesses place no value on the truth, at least if it doesn't serve their purposes, and they usually know when they are manipulating, deceiving, hurting, or lying to others. They stand in contrast to those with schizophrenia, bipolar disorder, clinical depression, panic disorder, post-traumatic stress disorder, and obsessive compulsive disorder, who may acknowledge reality as it is but may be helpless to revise their distorted beliefs. These mental illnesses can make critical thinking, at least about some issues, utterly impossible, even when the patient is receiving treatment.

You can acquaint your students with psychological defense mechanisms and increase their awareness of occasions when they are likely to use them, but you cannot do anything to mitigate personality disorders and other serious mental illnesses.

9. Critical Thinking Requires New Vocabulary

Students learning critical thinking will need to understand and speak the vocabulary of critical thinking: the verbs that refer to the cognitive operations that critical thinking involves, the logical fallacies that relate to your course material, and possibly even the dispositions and intellectual traits that critical thinking both requires and fosters. This vocabulary won't be as strange as a foreign language might be, but in some cases, students will have to exchange their everyday or mistaken understandings of the words for the academic definitions. Chapter 5 treats this topic in greater depth. It also offers techniques for teaching vocabulary that students will probably enjoy.

10. Critical Thinking Requires Students to Respond to Questions

To acquire critical thinking skills, students must answer questions that will make them think critically—that is, interpret, analyze, and evaluate course material. Leading up to such questions that demand high-level thinking, they may have to answer lower-level questions—to recall, to summarize, or to paraphrase material—to get everyone on the same page.

Instructors often find it challenging to motivate students to answer *any* questions, let alone those requiring high-level thinking. In addition, students will soon figure out that they may very well get a follow-up question like "How did you arrive at your response?" Most students do not enjoy being asked or having to answer either academic or reflective questions. Yet they need to participate because, as chapter 7 documents, discussion ranks first among all methods for fostering critical thinking (Abrami et al., 2014).

Moreover, students resist making their responses public because this involves genuine risk. First, they are breaking the norm of silence and passivity that governs most live and virtual classrooms, as well as the accompanying norm of the "consolidation of responsibility" for discussion in the talkative few (Howard, 2015, p. 48). Another related norm is that of "civil attention," (Howard, 2015, p. 12) where students feel they need only *appear* to be paying attention while their minds wander. As the instructor, you have to counter these norms by instituting and enforcing different norms that require all students to actively listen and participate (Howard, 2015). Second, some students shoulder additional risk because they are introverted, unacquainted with the nature of discussion, or of an opinion that runs counter to those already expressed. They abstain from participation and may feel marginalized or resentful as a result (Herman & Nilson, 2018). Third and perhaps most obviously, many students do not contribute because they fear giving a "wrong" answer, whether you or their peers pass the judgment. What if you put them down and shame them? What if other students make tittering noises or roll their eyes?

Besides, many students fail to see the connection between their answering questions and their learning. Why should that be necessary, they wonder, when you the instructor know all the answers? Why don't you just give us the answers? Why subject us to this meaningless exercise? This thinking typifies students at Perry's dualist and multiplicity stages and Wolcott's confused factfinder and biased jumper steps, and many students find themselves in those early phases of intellectual maturity.

You can alleviate some of students' struggles with speaking up in class or contributing to a discussion forum with a few easy strategies: Create a positive classroom or online course climate by maintaining an optimistic attitude; encouraging reaffirming interactions between your students; and ensuring fairness, equity, and inclusive course content (Ambrose et al., 2010). Tell students that discussion facilitates their developing critical thinking skills more effectively than any other class activity. Ask open-ended questions that have multiple good answers. In the live or remote classroom, wait at least 5 to 10 seconds before calling on anyone so that more students can have the time they need to think and formulate an answer. Let students test out and refine their responses in small groups before sharing them with the wider class.

Reassure them that you appreciate all well-intended participation, but ethically you can't allow erroneous answers to stand without correction, whether by you or other students. Set ground rules, perhaps in concert with your class, especially for discussing sensitive or controversial topics—for example, students should support their position with evidence and address their peers with respect and courtesy. Keep the exchange focused on the topic at hand. For variety, try engaging discussion-like formats such as the symposium, the press conference, the panel discussion, or small-group conversations.

Books on leading good discussions (e.g., Brookfield & Preskill, 2005, 2016; Herman & Nilson, 2018; Howard, 2015) provide hundreds of techniques and tips to induce students to talk in class, contribute to discussion boards, and answer high-level thinking questions. Appendix A in this book, Discussion Activities for Various Purposes, reprints brief descriptions of dozens of strategies from Herman and Nilson (2018)—specifically, ways for motivating students to prepare for discussion, to listen actively during discussion, and to contribute to a discussion.

Conclusion

Teaching critical thinking presents challenges unlike teaching other skills. To do it well, it requires targeted faculty development, explicit intention, subject matter amenable to high-level thinking, new vocabulary, and students who are self-regulating, of good character, emotionally healthy, ready for a challenging learning process, and up to answering a barrage of thought-provoking questions. This list may make teaching critical thinking sound impossible, but it isn't.

In chapter 4, you will begin to integrate critical thinking into your courses by formulating suitable student learning outcomes that make sense in your discipline and do not require you to redesign your current courses from scratch. This groundwork process will help you explicate your intention to teach critical thinking and include the appropriate subject matter in your courses. Chapters 5 through 7 will home in on how you can meet the daunting challenges of teaching critical thinking by providing students with instructional foundations, fostering their metacognitive awareness, presenting them with critical thinking questions, and leading them through specific learning activities and experiences. At that point, we will be primed to consider assessment strategies—objective items in chapter 8, constructed-response prompts in chapter 9, and two different approaches to assessing students' constructed responses in chapters 10 and 11.

4

FORMULATING CRITICAL
THINKING LEARNING
OUTCOMES

Student learning outcomes provide the foundation, the grounding, the skeleton for each of your courses. The outcomes should inform your teaching methods because some methods are more effective than others for helping students achieve certain types of outcomes (Davis & Arend, 2013; Nilson, 2016b). In addition, they should dictate your assessments because you should assess exactly what you want your students to be able to do at various junctures in your course. Formulate your outcomes, and the rest of your course unfolds on its own.

Infusing critical thinking into a course starts with developing critical thinking outcomes. You may have some of these among your current learning outcomes but perhaps haven't perceived or called them as such. If this is the case, integrating critical thinking into a course may require little of your time and effort. You should not have to redesign and restructure the course unless you have been requiring your students to exercise only low levels of thinking, such as memorization, basic translation, or plug-and-chug problem-solving.

In chapter 3, we established that major critical thinking scholars agree that you need subject matter that demands higher-level thinking in order to teach critical thinking and, therefore, a disciplinary course furnishes the best context. Other scholars such as Bonwell (2012), Schlueter (2016), and Willingham (2007, 2019) concur. This raises the question: Is critical thinking discipline-specific or the same across disciplines? Yes, it is the same across disciplines, but if you think about your courses only in terms of the eight general critical thinking skills that Facione (2020) and his Delphi group identified—interpretation, explanation, analysis, inference, evaluation, deduction, induction, and numeracy—or Elder and Paul's (2007) 10 universal intellectual standards—clarity, accuracy, precision, relevance, significance, completeness (or sufficiency), depth, breadth, logic, and fairness—you don't receive much direction. The wording and context of critical thinking outcomes, skills, and assessments differ across disciplines. As Willingham (2019) explains:

> Wanting students to be able to "analyse, synthesise, and evaluate" information sounds like a reasonable goal, but analysis, synthesis, and evaluation mean different things in different disciplines. Literary criticism has its own internal logic, its norms for what constitutes good evidence and a valid argument. These norms differ from those found in mathematics. And indeed, different domains—science and history, say—have different definitions on what it means to "know" something. Thus, our goals for student critical thinking must be domain-specific. An overarching principle like "think logically" is not a useful goal. (p. 6)

In addition, it is easier for you to consider how to incorporate critical thinking into your courses using your discipline's vocabulary and milieus. Therefore, the next several sections list possible critical thinking outcomes and skills for various disciplinary clusters. These lists do not exhaust all the possible outcomes for your courses, but they traverse a lot of learning terrain.

Critical Thinking Outcomes/Skills for the Sciences

If you teach a course that approaches phenomena from a scientific perspective, your discipline probably falls within the natural, physical, mathematical, social, psychological, or applied sciences. It relies on the scientific method, and you probably want your students to be able to practice some facets of this method.

We can turn to physics for initial guidance as well as for validation of the disciplinary cluster approach taken here. The Rutgers Physics and Astronomy Education (2014; Etkina et al., 2006) group has developed a list of scientific abilities/skills, which also suggest physics course outcomes:

- Design and conduct an observational experiment, including deciding the variables to be measured and how to measure them.
- Design and conduct a testing experiment, including deciding the variables to be measured and how to measure them.
- Design and conduct an application experiment, including deciding the variables to be measured and how to measure them.

- Gather and analyze experimental data.
- Represent information, data, or findings in multiple ways.
- Evaluate equations, solutions, models, and claims.
- Communicate scientific ideas clearly.

These skills represent calculus-based, undergraduate-level, lab-oriented physics but do not encompass every learning outcome across the STEM fields. We should add them to a more comprehensive list. The outcomes following may make good candidates for you to consider or adapt to your course, whatever your STEM discipline. You might check those that apply to your courses:

- Identify problems using data.
- Recognize and explain a problem, position, or question.
- Classify problems by their types and the correct algorithms to solve them.
- Solve problems using data from multiple sources.
- Design and conduct an observational experiment, including deciding the variables to be measured and how to measure them.
- Design and conduct a testing experiment, including deciding the variables to be measured and how to measure them.
- Design and conduct an application experiment, including deciding the variables to be measured and how to measure them.
- Gather and analyze experimental data.
- Represent information, data, or findings in multiple ways.
- Evaluate models, equations, solutions, and claims.
- Evaluate different solutions and select the best one(s).
- Describe how new data or information may require a new definition of a problem, a revised hypothesis, or a different solution.
- Assess the consistency of hypotheses with known facts.
- Assess the consistency of data with known facts or hypotheses.
- Select, justify, and carry out appropriate methodologies (experimental, survey, interviews) for testing a hypothesis.
- Appraise the methodologies that others selected for their studies.
- Formulate and defend one's positions, hypotheses, findings, or interpretations.
- Analyze and explain the limitations of one's positions, hypotheses, findings, or interpretations.
- Make sense of quantitative relationships expressed statistically (specify which statistics).

- Make sense of quantitative relationships displayed in graphs, charts, tables, and other graphics.
- Express quantitative relationships statistically (specify which statistics).
- Show quantitative relationships in graphs, charts, tables, and other graphics.
- Distinguish possible spurious from causal relationships.
- Explain the problems with drawing conclusions from correlational relationships in the data.
- Identify and evaluate alternative interpretations of the data or observations, including competing causal explanations.
- Explain the implications of given research findings.
- Explain the significance of given research findings to a line of research, a subspecialty, or the discipline as a whole.
- Isolate and assess the assumptions and contextual influences behind one's own and others' positions.
- Distinguish facts from inferences and opinions.
- Assess the relevance of given information to appraise an argument or conclusion.
- Analyze arguments for the strength of their evidence, their internal consistency, and their logic.
- Communicate scientific ideas clearly.

Of the skills/outcomes you checked as applicable to your courses, you may want to add specifics to them. For instance, if you'd like your students to be able to solve problems using data from multiple sources, you might specify those sources, such as academic journals, certain websites, and data obtained from a lab experiment. Or, if you want your students to learn how to explain the implications of given research findings, you might want to designate the kind of implications—for example, for further research, for the discipline's direction, or for some practical application. Of course, do add any outcomes you have in mind that didn't make the preceding list.

Critical Thinking Outcomes/Skills for the Technical and Problem-Solving Disciplines

Technical and problem-solving fields have grown out of the natural, physical, mathematical, and psychological sciences to address problems that humans encounter. Therefore, many of their critical thinking outcomes/ skills overlap with those of the sciences—certainly those skills that include the word "problem" or "solution." These specialties span all areas of business, engineering, computer science, counseling, human and veterinary medicine, nursing, the allied health fields, and a range of technical subjects. They, too, require their students to learn how to:

- Identify problems using data.
- Recognize and explain a problem, position, or question.
- Classify problems by their types and the correct algorithms to solve them.
- Solve problems using data from multiple sources.
- Evaluate different solutions and select the best one(s).
- Describe how new data or information may require a new definition of a problem or a different solution.
- Select, justify, and carry out appropriate methodologies for studying or solving a problem.
- Appraise the methodologies that others selected.
- Formulate and defend one's positions, hypotheses, findings, or interpretations.
- Analyze and explain the limitations of one's positions, hypotheses, findings, or interpretations.
- Make sense of quantitative relationships expressed statistically (specify which statistics).
- Make sense of quantitative relationships displayed in graphs, charts, tables, and other graphics.
- Express quantitative relationships statistically (specify which statistics).
- Show quantitative relationships in graphs, charts, tables, and other graphics.

Practitioners in these fields must also take into account certain pragmatic matters of concern to a client or employer, so we should add this critical thinking outcome/skill:

- Evaluate different problem definitions, solutions, or conclusions and select the best one(s) taking into consideration cost, time, feasibility, and client/patient preferences.

Critical Thinking Outcomes/Skills for the Rhetorical Disciplines

Here, I am using *rhetorical* to mean "verbal" in both the written and the oral sense of the term. Encompassing the humanities, oratory (public speaking), law, and certain subareas of the social sciences (e.g., theory, ethnography), these disciplines create and critique arguments that are based on qualitative data sources such as texts, key observations, documents, artifacts, and logic. (Law also draws on scientific evidence to make a case.) Their critical thinking outcomes include these, the first six of which echo some in the sciences:

- Isolate and assess the assumptions and contextual influences behind one's own and others' positions.
- Recognize and explain a position or argument.
- Distinguish facts from inferences and opinions.
- Assess the relevance of given information to appraise an argument or conclusion.
- Analyze arguments for the strength of their evidence, their internal consistency, and their logic.
- Analyze and explain the limitations of one's own arguments and interpretations.
- Find and draw on relevant primary and secondary sources to conduct research.
- Examine and evaluate arguments to explain historical and contemporary problems, events, issues, and trends (Nuhfer et al., 2014).
- Develop arguments to explain historical and contemporary problems, events, issues, and trends (Nuhfer et al., 2014).
- Assess competing interpretations, evidence, arguments, explanations, and conclusions.
- Communicate complex ideas clearly and convincingly.

Critical Thinking Outcomes/Skills for the Arts

Finally, we turn to the arts: the visual and graphic arts, music, dance, drama, theater, film, and creative writing (poetry, plays, short stories, novelettes, and novels). They strive to help a student achieve their own distinctive learning outcomes—for example:

- Identify themes or important features in works of art.
- Interpret and critique a work following commonly agreed-upon criteria.
- Analyze other interpretations of a work.
- Evaluate interpretations of a work against the evidence contained in the work.
- Analyze a range of works to document growth or changes in an artist or across locations, cultures, or historical periods.

- Infer the historical period, location, school, artist, and motivation of given works (Nuhfer et al., 2014).
- Identify analyses and critiques of specific works as subjective or objective.
- Create or perform a satisfactory (or better) work of art and explicate its significance.

Self-Regulated Learning Outcomes/Skills

While it may be challenging to design a course that explicitly develops good character and intellectual virtues (see chapter 5 for how you can), we certainly can design one that equips students with self-regulated learning skills. Self-regulated learning is all about self-awareness, self-observation, and self-assessment. Given that these skills must accompany critical thinking, a course with a critical thinking emphasis should have some self-regulated learning outcomes for students as well. Here are just a few suggestions (Nilson, 2013):

- Develop, experiment with, and assess learning strategies connected with critical thinking tasks.
- Set goals for defining success in completing a learning task requiring critical thinking.
- Identify the key points (or the most important, valuable, useful, or surprising points) in readings, videos, podcasts, or lectures.
- Tie new knowledge and skills to prior learning or experiences.
- Set goals and preparation strategies to improve one's performance on exams and assignments.
- Observe, analyze, and articulate one's thinking process in arriving at a response or solution.
- Analyze how one develops, evaluates, and narrows down alternative solutions to complex problems.
- Diagnose and solve the reasoning or research problems that one encounters while completing an assignment.
- Monitor and communicate, orally and in writing, one's critical thinking while doing course activities and assignments (reading, watching, listening, writing, designing, organizing, doing field work or service-learning tasks, performing in a role-play or simulation, etc.).
- Develop strategies on how to best apply instructor and peer feedback to revise a paper or project involving critical thinking.

- Evaluate one's progress in applying critical thinking in not only academic but also everyday situations.
- Predict useful ways to apply one's newly acquired critical thinking skills beyond the course.
- Analyze how and why learning and using critical thinking in this course has changed one's attitudes, behaviors, beliefs, values, world view, and habits of mind.

As you present such learning outcomes to your students, do explain what self-regulated learning is. In general, it is learning how to learn by being self-aware of what one is and isn't learning, but, more specifically, it is the conscious planning, monitoring, and evaluation of one's learning for the purpose of maximizing it. Plenty of research documents that self-regulated learning increases the amount and the quality of a student's learning and motivation to learn, which in turn enhances academic performance and college persistence (Nilson, 2013).

You can engage your students in practicing self-regulated learning and experiencing its benefits by leading them in certain activities and making certain assignments—specifically, ones in which they reflect on how they can best plan and strategize their learning, how they are progressing through their learning process, and how they evaluate their learning and their learning strategies at the end. These activities and assignments can occur at the beginning and end of a course; occasionally during a course; or in conjunction with typical course components, such as readings (or videos or podcasts), live or recorded lectures, assignments, quizzes, and major exams (Nilson, 2013). The activities require no grading at all, and almost all the assignments need only a quick pass/fail assessment based on completion and your mandatory minimum length (number of words). A "pass" earns a student credit or some nominal number of points; a "fail" earns no credit or points and goes to a work that is incomplete or too brief. Nilson (2013) gives much more guidance and suggests dozens of possible activities and assignments, most of them very short, simple to implement, content-reinforcing, and unobjectionable to students.

Conclusion

Your learning outcomes provide the starting point, road map, and destination of your course. If you hope your students leave your course with any critical thinking skills, you should formulate some critical thinking outcomes. Because meaningful critical thinking outcomes grow out of your discipline, they may already be "hidden" in your list of current course outcomes, requiring only minor modification and labeling as "critical thinking" skills. However, you may have to add self-regulated learning outcomes along with some suitable activities and assignments to develop those skills. Self-regulated learning does not take away time or focus from your subject matter. It only helps your students learn it better.

5

FOSTERING YOUR STUDENTS' COGNITIVE AWARENESS TO TEACH CRITICAL THINKING

W

e know that critical thinking skills can be taught, despite the fact that teaching them is a challenging endeavor. We also know that students learn these skills more effectively when instructors receive advance training or coaching in teaching critical thinking and provide students with plenty of opportunity to practice these skills on varied content (Willingham, 2007). If you cannot find a source of in-depth training or coaching, applying the advice in this chapter and chapters 6 and 7 can greatly enhance your students' chances of becoming critical thinkers in your courses.

This chapter will help you accomplish two goals: (a) It will aid in acquainting your students with critical thinking so that they understand what it "looks like" and entails, and (b) it will enable you to enhance their self-awareness of their own thinking so that they know when they are and are not thinking critically. The first two sections will help you provide a foundation for your students—specifically giving them the vocabulary for doing critical thinking and watching you do critical thinking. The latter two sections will enable you to help your students acquire the flexible and self-scrutinizing mindset that allows for critical thinking. Indeed, critical thinking is a metacognitive, self-regulated activity.

Familiarize Students With the New Vocabulary

In chapter 3, we established that teaching critical thinking requires intentional and explicit infusion into a course, or students won't acquire the skills

(Abrami et al., 2008; Burbach et al., 2004; Edwards, 2017; Paul et al., 2013). To do so, they must learn to use the vocabulary of critical thinking, including the cognitive operations involved in critical thinking, the logical fallacies that thwart it, and the objects of critical thinking: claims.

Most of us assume that our students know the meaning of the thinking verbs we use so casually, but they may not. Part of dispelling their misconceptions about the nature of critical thinking entails "translating" its verbs into easy-to-remember lay language that they can grasp. These terms are more esoteric than we may think. For instance:

- To *interpret* means to figure out, identify, explain, clarify, decipher, or elucidate the meaning or intention of an author's statement/quotation.
- To *analyze* means to examine, explore, investigate, or inspect, or most specifically, to dissect/pull apart/break into constituent parts, such as an event into its causes, a theory into its assumptions and deductions, or a process into its steps/stages, and then explaining how the parts interrelate; it can also mean to recount the progress or course of a trend, phenomenon, or development; it can also mean to categorize, classify, or group concepts, parts, or examples by their key characteristics.
- To *evaluate* means to assess, judge, appraise, critique, review, or determine either the value of something or the degree to which it measures up to certain criteria or standards; it can also mean to validate, prove, or disprove—that is, to establish the truth or falsity of a claim by providing factual evidence or sound, logical reasons.

Few of our students have even heard of logical fallacies, let alone know how to identify them. Most of us are familiar with just a sampling, such as the hasty generalization, straw man, slippery slope, red herring, and *ad hominem.* In fact, Williamson (2018) lists and defines almost 150 logical fallacies. You might visit his site to identify those related to your subject matter—that is, those that may appear in your students' course readings or videos or future disciplinary studies. In addition to defining these fallacies in class, you might give your students practice in identifying them in the mass media, social media, or reading or video assignments. You might even situate this practice in a find-the-fallacy game.

Finally, critical thinking starts with the appropriate subject matter, which is a *claim.* Chapter 3 first defined it as a belief, a value, a disputed definition or fact, a definition of a problem, an interpretation, an assumption, an explanation, a hypothesis, prediction, a theory, solution, an analysis, an argument, a justification, a judgment, an evaluation, a critique, a generalization, an inference, an implication, a contention, an opinion, a viewpoint, a position, a decision, or a conclusion—some sort of statement that is disputed, debated, controversial, suspect, or uncertain. As with fallacies, students can benefit from some practice distinguishing claims from undisputed definitions, facts, and conventions.

Model Critical Thinking for Your Students

Before students can solve a problem, perform a procedure, transfer knowledge to new situations, or engage in any sophisticated thought processes, they need to watch or listen to you do it. That is, you need to model the process for them—live, in a teleconference, or in a video. They must witness *you* interpreting and analyzing claims, issues, and problems out loud; asking yourself questions about the source and validity of your own claims; and grappling with uncertainty and tentativeness. And they should feel safe asking you questions and expressing skepticism about your answers. In addition, you should model the proper attitudes, dispositions, and character traits—intellectual humility, integrity, curiosity, fair-mindedness, willingness to change one's thinking, and the like (Edwards, 2017; Facione, 1990, 2011; Facione et al., 2000; Halpern, 1999; Paul & Elder, 2014).

In their team-taught course, Religion in American Life and Thought, Seesholtz and Polk (2009) modeled civil debate as well as critical thinking in front of their class. With Seesholtz being a critic of the doctrine-based politics of organized religion and Polk being a chaplain at Abington College, their disagreements ran deep. Still, these two scholars demonstrated the value of debate in enhancing mutual understanding of the opposing point of view, evaluating the validity of both points of view, and deepening one's perspective on the issue. If you do not have a colleague to debate with during your class, consider conducting a debate with yourself to show your students how they, too, may debate with themselves.

Integrate Reflective Prompts Into Critical Thinking Activities and Assignments

Monitoring and evaluating one's thinking—that is, reflection to foster self-awareness—is an essential component of critical thinking. Therefore, it's important for you to incorporate reflective prompts into the critical thinking activities and assignments that chapters 6, 7, and 9 describe (Edwards, 2017; Facione, 2020). As you plan an activity or assignment, make one or more of these prompts an integral part of it.

For example, in face-to-face or online discussions, have students *routinely* justify their answers, solutions, or conclusions by asking, "How did you arrive at your response?" After students get used to hearing this question again and again, they will be well prepared to answer it whether or not you explicitly pose it. As they frame their responses to questions, they will observe themselves thinking through the task.

In addition to asking students to self-monitor, you can give short writing assignments, such as 3-minute free writes or self-regulated learning exercises associated with readings, videos, podcasts, live, teleconferenced, or recorded lectures, quizzes and exams, problem sets, experiential learning activities, and substantial content-focused assignments such as papers and projects. Their goal is to build students' self-awareness through reflection. These self-regulated learning exercises are called "wrappers" because they "wrap around" other course activities and assessments. Some of the simplest reflection probes ask students to identify the idea(s) in a reading, video, or podcast that they considered the most important, the most useful, the most surprising, or the most difficult to understand. Or to describe their affective reactions to the material. Or to connect what they learned to their prior knowledge or other disciplines or courses (Nilson, 2013).

In a more elaborate reflection task, students draw an appropriate graphic representing a reading, video, podcast, or lecture. If the material describes a process, procedure, or sequence of events, a flowchart would probably serve best. If it focuses on classifying or comparing and contrasting different events, people, objects, or phenomena, a matrix would be most suitable. For portraying hierarchical relationships among concepts, categories, principles, or subjects, a concept map or a mind map would best fit the task. If the material pertains to other kinds of relationships, such as overlaps in observations or examples, you might have your students create a concept circle diagram (e.g., a Venn diagram). When students create a graphic, they have to reflect on how they visualize the relationships in their mind and, therefore, how to structure and integrate the knowledge. This process deepens learning, promotes conceptual understanding, ensures longer-term retention, and facilitates retrieval (Robinson et al., 1998; Robinson & Kiewra, 1995; Vekiri, 2002).

Some forms of journaling also qualify as self-regulated learning assignments, such as those that ask students to record changes in their learning strategies, their perceptions of their growth or improvements in course skills, and their affective reactions to the course material (e.g., modifications in their values, beliefs, or opinions and the sources of these modifications) (Nilson, 2013).

For mathematics-based problem-solving assignments, students need to know whether they understand new material deeply enough to apply it to

the problems. Often they think they do because the textbook and your explanations seemed so crystal clear, but then the homework problems stump
them. To help them find out before they try to tackle the homework alone,
let students work in pairs on the first two problems in class. In an activity
called "Think Aloud," one student articulates their approach to solving the
first problem, while the other gives guidance and feedback as needed; for the
second problem, the partners switch roles (Lockhead & Whimbey, 1987).
Another strategy makes the best use of errors in problem-solving by having
the students learn from them—specifically, having them write out an error
analysis of where they went wrong and then solving the same or a similar
problem correctly, with peer or instructor help (Zimmerman et al., 2011).

Tests furnish yet another opportunity for reflection and self-regulation.
After you return a graded exam, have students (a) learn from their mistakes
by correctly solving the problems they missed or performing the tasks they
did poorly (The Self-Regulated Learning Program, n.d.; Zimmerman et al.,
2011) or (b) reflect on why they lost points, how effectively they prepared,
and how they will prepare better for the next exam (Achacoso, 2004: Barkley,
2009). Both these activities can take place in or out of class.

In-class activities need not be graded at all, and short to medium-size
assignments need only be graded pass/fail, credit/no-credit, some number
of points or no points. When your students answer all the prompts and
meet the minimum word length that you designate, that work merits a pass
(Nilson, 2013). This type of "grading" takes little or no time.

Papers, projects, and essay test answers—called constructed responses
later in this book—also deserve and create rich opportunities for reflection.
We will reserve discussing reflective prompts for these until chapter 9 (this
volume), which focuses on how to design constructed-response questions
and tasks to assess critical thinking.

Foster Good Character in Your Students

How can you induce your students to acquire good character and specifically the intellectual virtues, traits, and dispositions that critical thinking
requires? While the literature explicates those virtues, traits, and dispositions
(see chapter 2, this volume), it offers little advice to instructors who aim to
cultivate them in students.

Fortunately, some of the strategies for teaching critical thinking in themselves foster these dispositions and traits. Most helpful among the activities
earlier in this chapter are your explicit modeling and having students reflect
on their thinking and justify their responses. Self-regulated learning activities

and assignments can help build three of Halpern's (2015) four dispositions—namely, persisting at a task, self-disciplined planning, and exchanging erroneous approaches for better ones. Once students begin to acquire the conducive dispositions and traits, their motivation to think critically will increase and their thinking skills will improve, further fostering the desired dispositions and traits. Students will start to appreciate the benefits of critical thinking and its accompanying qualities of character.

In chapters 6 and 7 we will examine additional strategies that can promote good character, such as having students answer certain critical thinking questions (e.g., those asking to generate or evaluate multiple interpretations or viewpoints), having them discuss a multifaceted issue, having them debrief cases (especially when following Brookfield's scenario analysis), and moving students through Perry's (1968), Elder and Paul's (2010), or Wolcott's (2006) developmental models. More on these strategies later.

Assigning your students certain books or parts of them represents another strategy. Especially through narrative fiction, students can acquaint themselves with people who have good (or bad) character or otherwise demonstrate intellectual virtues and dispositions (or their opposite) (Nussbaum, 1997; Schwartz, 2015). The novel *Siddhartha* (Hesse, 1951) exemplifies such a book. It is a fictional account of the spiritual journey of Siddhārtha Gautama through his early adult life as he sought enlightenment and eventually became The Buddha. It traces his struggle to find truth, including his critical thinking processes, as he tried different avenues—joining the ascetic Samanas and following Gotoma and then pursuing business and materialism, which turned out to be just a game to him. Finally, he found himself studying the river, where he realized the interconnectedness of all life. Although the historical Siddhārtha Gautama started out life as wealthy nobility and reputedly realized enlightenment sitting under a Bodhi tree, the book reflects the man's life pretty closely. In addition, as a novel, it can portray his inner thoughts and reflections as a biography cannot.

Still, many biographies and autobiographies offer another channel for students to learn about character and the intellectual struggles that people striving to do the right thing persevere through. Foner's (2010) biography of Abraham Lincoln, classified as historical nonfiction, tracks Lincoln's internal conflicts about slavery and Blacks during his presidency. Unbeknownst to most Americans, he changed his mind about such issues quite a few times during the Civil War.

Don't forget movies and television shows either. Students experience excellent models in *Lincoln* (2012), *Schindler's List* (1993) (the Schindler character), *Meet Joe Black* (1998) (the character of William Parrish, played by Anthony Hopkins), *The Lion King* (1994, 2019), *Erin Brockovich* (2000),

The Blind Side (2009), and *Free Willy: Escape from Pirate's Cove* (2010) (the Kirra character), to name just a few films. Many of your students have already watched some of these. For examples of bad character, it's difficult to beat Walter White in AMC's *Breaking Bad* (2008–2013) or Jordan Belfort in *The Wolf of Wall Street* (2013). There are helpful websites on films, such as 20 Inspirational Movies With Important Life Lessons (Reecekesson, 2019) and 25 of the Best Family Movies for Teaching Honesty, Grit, Courage & More (Ceynar, n.d.).

Conclusion

Teaching critical thinking starts with laying good groundwork for your students and encouraging them to cultivate intellectual virtues, such as their awareness of self. In introducing your students to critical thinking vocabulary, choose a sample of terms that students will need to know to complete a specific assignment, spot a problem in a misleading claim, or perform well on one or more of your exams. In other words, add to their vocabulary on a need-to-know basis.

For modeling critical thinking for your students, select a couple of exemplary problems or dilemmas during the term. Don't feeling obliged to model it on a regular basis in class or a video recording.

To encourage good character traits in your students, you can assign one or more fiction or nonfiction readings that demonstrate moral and intellectual virtues and dispositions. You might not be able to assign a movie or television show, but you can refer in class or online to model characters from popular media that your students have probably seen. You can also pique your students' recollection of characters who personify greed, selfishness, close-mindedness, imprudent decision-making, intellectual inflexibility, denial, faulty reasoning, narcissism, and poor impulse control. Such types usually pay for their crimes against truth.

Finally, "wrap" some reflective prompts around your course activities and assignments. Your modest efforts will not only reinforce your students' thinking skills but also help build your students' self-regulated learning abilities. These abilities greatly enhance academic success, especially among struggling students (Nilson, 2013; Visible Learning, 2017; Zimmerman et al., 2011). When you and your students see good results, you can confidently begin to add more reflections to your course activities and assignments.

6

ASKING YOUR STUDENTS THE RIGHT QUESTIONS TO TEACH CRITICAL THINKING

Having dealt with foundational issues in chapter 5, we are ready to tackle the core activity in teaching critical thinking, which is challenging students with the "right" questions—that is, those that demand and give practice in critical thinking. You can pose such questions within many different instructional activities and assignments: face-to-face and online discussions, case debriefings, debates, writing exercises, small-group work, short homework assignments, and long written assignments and projects. Take advantage of every chance you get. As stated in chapter 3, students must answer questions that will make them think critically to acquire critical thinking skills, and to learn any new, complex skill, they need repeated, varied practice (Edwards, 2017; Willingham, 2017). In a study conducted in an undergraduate research methods course, the instructors were able to advance their students' critical thinking skills, including inductive and deductive logic reasoning skills, just by asking a well-structured series of evaluative questions on the scholarly publications that the students gathered (Tremblay & Downey, 2004).

Writing, in particular, develops as well as demonstrates critical thinking. Bean (1996) calls it "the exterior sign of an interior thinking process" (p. 20). He also considers argumentative and analytical writing, which provides practice in critical thinking, the foundation of scholarly inquiry. Elder and Paul (2006) recognize the same "intimate connection" (p. 38) between the clarity of one's thinking and the quality of one's writing.

Questions Derived From Your Learning Outcomes

Your learning outcomes should guide your choice of questions and tasks. Students need practice, followed by feedback, in performing your learning outcomes. One very easy way to develop these prompts is to turn your critical thinking outcomes into questions and tasks. Usually, outcomes are already phrased like tasks. Of course, you will have to situate these prompts in the subject matter context of your course. Following are three examples for the basic and applied sciences, succeeded by a fourth example for the rhetorical disciplines and a fifth for the arts:

1. Outcome: Identify problems using data.
   Prompt: Examine these graphs about the income distributions and life expectancy in various societies. What social, health, and economic problems do the data reveal about (a) large, advanced capitalist nations and (b) developing nations?
2. Outcome: Solve problems using data from multiple sources.
   Prompt: Accompanied by his mother, a male child comes to the ER presenting a temperature of 101°F, severe muscle aches, and a persistent dry cough. In developing a diagnosis, what questions would you ask the patient? What questions would you ask the mother? What would you look for in the patient's medical history? What tests might you order and why?
3. Outcome: Formulate and defend one's positions, hypotheses, and interpretations.
   Prompt: What patterns, if any, do you see in this data set? If you do discern patterns, what hypotheses do they suggest? Which ones are worth conducting a study to test? Why?
4. Outcome: Distinguish facts from inferences and opinions.
   Prompt: In this brief literary analysis, which statements are accurate descriptions of the text, and which are interpretations or inferences?
5. Outcome: Infer the historical period, location, school, artist, and motivation of given works.
   Prompt: Consider this dark, sinister painting titled *Abduction*. Who was the artist? At what time in his or her career did he or she paint it? In about what year? What struggle was the artist experiencing at the time? With what school is he or she associated?

To teach critical thinking and give students practice doing it, let us also consider the questions and tasks that the leading critical thinking scholars suggest. While these questions (paraphrased from the authors' works) are general and not discipline-linked, they may help you better phrase your own prompts and even think of outcomes and questions that haven't occurred to you before. Because the list of questions and tasks is long to the point of unruly, I have synthesized and collapsed them into one list near the end of this chapter.

Brookfield's Questions

Brookfield (2012b) suggests a series of critical thinking questions to pose to students.

Questions to detect the assumptions in an author's/researcher's work (remember Brookfield's broad definition of *assumptions*):

- Can you identify any assumptions that the author/researcher seems to be operating under?
- What cause-and-effect relationship(s) is the author/researcher suggesting?
- What do you think is the most accurate assumption in this work, and where in the work do you find it?

Questions to evaluate the evidence behind these assumptions:

- What is the most convincing/persuasive piece of evidence in support of a conclusion that that the author/researcher gives?
- What is the least persuasive piece of evidence given?
- What is the best supported argument or conclusion?
- What would be the most powerful evidence to a skeptic?

Questions to generate alternative interpretations or explanations:

- How would [another specific author/researcher] approach the problem?
- What perspective or approach does the work not include? If it did include it, how would the work be different?
- If different data were included, how would the research be different?
- Do you think that the author/researcher purposely excluded any perspective or data?
- What questions or issues are still unresolved?

Questions to focus students on their own thinking:

- What assumption are you making that you're the most confident about? The least confident about?
- What is an example of your assumption/point?

- _____ seems to be an explicit assumption that you are making. What might be an implicit assumption that you hold?
- What do you mean? Explain the term you just used.
- How do you know _____? What data/evidence do you have to justify it?
- What data/evidence are you most confident about?
- How would you counter a skeptic?
- How would [a specific author/researcher] react to your analysis?
- What idea/argument/evidence might you have missed or left out? Whose views/work might you have forgotten or ignored?

Facione's Questions

Facione (2020) recommends asking students critical thinking questions like the ones following, grouped by thinking skill.

- *Interpretation*: What does this mean? What sense can we make of it? What do you think the author/researcher intended by it?
- *Analysis*: How can you justify your conclusion? What assumptions underlie your conclusion? What are competing arguments? If they imply different conclusions, how can you reconcile them?
- *Inference*: What are the implications of this evidence/these data? What are the implications of this assumption? How about the unintended consequences? What conclusions can we eliminate? What alternate conclusions should we examine? What else do we need to know?
- *Evaluation*: To what extent does this claim/argument accurately represent the evidence/data? What logical flaws lead you to question the argument? How much trust does the source merit? How much confidence does the conclusion justify?
- *Explanation*: What are the key findings of this study/research? How sound is the analysis? How sound is the solution/conclusion? How sound and comprehensive are the limitations given?

Halpern's Tasks

Following are Halpern's (1999) critical thinking tasks to assign to students.

- Analyze an argument to distill and evaluate its assumptions.
- Define the problems in a situation.
- Connect new with prior knowledge.
- Lay out a step-by-step plan for achieving a goal.

- Articulate reasons to defend or dismiss a claim.
- Estimate the probability of a possible occurrence or result.
- Contextualize data into a wider perspective.
- Translate text-based content into a visual.
- Integrate data/information from disparate sources.
- Examine options to select the best one.

Elder and Paul's Questions

Elder and Paul (2007) provide templates of questions for different purposes, but all these templates show students how to practice critical thinking—interpreting, analyzing, and evaluating key ideas—in reading assignments. The set in the following numbered list is designed to hold students accountable for meeting the 10 intellectual standards for critical thinking. The hope is for students to internalize and ask themselves these questions in other classes and in everyday life.

1. *Clarity*: Can you elaborate and phrase your point more specifically? Perhaps give an example? Elder and Paul (2007) call clarity the gateway standard because we cannot apply the other standards to a claim without understanding it.
2. *Accuracy*: What evidence can you provide for your statement? What backup can you lend your evidence?
3. *Precision*: What greater detail or specificity can you provide?
4. *Relevance*: What is the relevance of that information to the issue?
5. *Significance*: What is the most important/central problem or idea? Which information is most important?
6. *Completeness* (or *Sufficiency*): To what extent have you gathered all the information possible to justify your solution/conclusion?
7. *Depth*: How does your solution deal with the most central and complex facets of the problem? What about viability and compromised values?
8. *Breadth*: What other perspectives can you offer on the issue? Can you represent the opposing side?
9. *Logic*: How does the evidence or prior claims lead you to this conclusion? How can both these claims be valid when they lead to different conclusions?
10. *Fairness*: To what extent are you biased in favor one result/conclusion or another? How objectively and honestly can you explain other perspectives?

The next set of eight questions is intended to guide students' analyses of articles, essays, chapters, and textbooks:

1. What is the main purpose/intention of the text/author?
2. What is the key question that the text/author tries to answer?
3. What is the most important information/evidence the text/author furnishes to support the conclusions?
4. What are the text/author's major conclusions or inferences?
5. What are the text/author's major lines of reasoning?
6. What are the text/author's major assumptions?
7. What are the text/author's logical implications, whether stated or not, of the line of reasoning?
8. What is the text/author's primary point of view?

Elder and Paul (2007) offer the final set of eight questions to help students evaluate parts of a text:

1. How well expressed and justified is the author's purpose/intention?
2. How clearly and impartially stated, relevant to the purpose, and true to the complexities is the key question?
3. How accurate, relevant, essential, and true to the complexities is the key information/are the key data?
4. How clear and are the key justifiable are the major ideas?
5. How valid are the assumptions? To what extent does the author address their limitations?
6. How logically derived are the conclusions and inferences from the information/data given?
7. To what extent does the author acknowledge and challenge other perspectives or lines of reasoning?
8. To what extent does the author acknowledge the implications of the conclusions drawn and the inferences made?

Paul and Elder offer a great deal more material on teaching critical thinking, including assignments for students, at the Foundation for Critical Thinking (n.d.). However, access requires paid membership in the Critical Thinking Community.

Wolcott's Assignment Prompts

Wolcott (2006) provides sets of assignment tasks to help students move from step 0 to step 4 on her thinking ladder. Students will need practice responding to these prompts on different problems, cases, articles, books, situations, pieces of literature, and the like.

To move students from the confused fact-finder to the biased jumper step, you can give students practice in basic thinking skills such as identifying problems, the relevant information, and uncertainties related to the problem. Here are some possible prompts based on Wolcott's work:

- Identify different points of view or relevant information for exploring a given issue. Why is there disagreement?
- Identify the perspectives or claims that lack the evidence to be known with certainty.
- Explain why a certain occurrence cannot be predicted with confidence.
- Explain the sources of uncertainty.
- List the issues or information related to a given problem or concern.
- Identify several possible solutions to a problem.
- Identify the evidence that warrants each possible solution.

Students who can articulate solid responses to the prompts in the preceding list advance to the biased jumper performance pattern. To help them progress to the perpetual analyzer step, you can offer more complex prompts that require interpretation and argument analysis from multiple perspectives:

- Interpret information/findings from multiple points of view.
- Compare and contrast the arguments behind multiple points of view or solutions.
- Assess the evidence behind multiple points of view or solutions.
- Explain the assumptions and their implications behind multiple points of view or solutions.
- Explain the implications of your own assumptions, experiences, and point of view on a given issue.

Once students can comfortably perform the tasks in the previous list, they achieve the perpetual analyzer pattern. Assigning the following questions will help them advance to the pragmatic performer step. These tasks include setting priorities for analyzing and choosing among options and tailoring communication to given audiences and settings.

- Propose and defend a solution/conclusion/plan/policy/ recommendation related to a given problem.
- Identify the criteria that you prioritized in developing your solution/ conclusion/plan/policy/recommendation.

- Justify your decision to prioritize certain criteria over other criteria.
- If you prioritized other criteria, explain how the solution/conclusion/plan/policy/recommendation might change.
- Predict the arguments you might hear in favor of other solutions/conclusions/plans/policies/recommendations.
- Articulate your responses to these arguments.
- Identify what a given audience would most want to learn about your solution/conclusion/plan/policy/recommendation.
- Explain the strategy you would use in your memo/report/presentation to reach and persuade this audience.
- Explain how you would change your strategy to reach and persuade different audiences.

When students can develop intelligent answers to these questions, they have matured into the pragmatic performer pattern. While an admirable landing, the following tasks will raise their awareness of the shortcomings of their approach or conclusion, motivating them to stand back, monitor the situation, seek new information, and stay open to revising their solution—the mindset of the strategic re-visioner.

- Evaluate the limitations of your solution/conclusion/plan/policy/recommendation.
- Identify the priorities or interests that your solution/conclusion/plan/policy/recommendation disregards or shortchanges.
- Explain what possible changes in the future would motivate you to reevaluate your solution/conclusion/plan/policy/recommendation.
- Identify ways for you to gather new information relevant to your solution/conclusion/plan/policy/recommendation.
- Develop a strategy for you to monitor the effectiveness of your solution/conclusion/plan/policy/recommendation.
- Develop a strategy for you to revisit the problem and possibly revise your solution/conclusion/plan/policy/recommendation in the future.

Not many students will be willing and able to reach the strategic re-visioner step. In Wolcott's framework, it is the most sophisticated performance pattern—one that demands self-discipline, integrity, courage, and emotional separation from one's work. These recall some of the intellectual traits, virtues, and dispositions that other scholars have forwarded as necessary for critical thinking. This performance pattern also characterizes excellent communicators who can explain their thinking to people from many walks of life.

Bonwell's Tasks

Charles Bonwell never wrote a book articulating a framework of critical thinking, but in 2012 he did publish a fairly influential article, "A Disciplinary Approach for Teaching Critical Thinking," that endorses teaching critical thinking in disciplinary courses. In its notes section at the end, he lists general thinking skills that echo those in the comprehensive critical thinking frameworks we have examined. Not to linger over his list, but in case the previous summaries left out any important questions or tasks, this list should cover them:

- Pose questions for clarification.
- Define a central issue or challenge.
- Classify or sequence data/information.
- Discern patterns in data/information/findings.
- Evaluate the credibility of a source.
- Separate fact from opinion.
- Identify ambiguities and uncertainties.
- Identify the stated and unstated assumptions, values, or reasons for conclusions.
- Identify instances of faulty reasoning (e.g., logical, statistical).
- Identify omitted information and considerations.
- Identify the conclusions as well as possible alternative conclusions.
- Articulate the compare-and-contrast and causal relationships between elements.
- Develop analogies to explain relationships or procedures.
- Project future trends or outcomes.
- Represent text material graphically and graphic material, verbally.

Synthesis of Questions/Tasks to Give Students Practice in Critical Thinking Skills

To facilitate your use of critical thinking questions and tasks, I have prepared a synthesized "master list" that captures just about all the previously listed prompts. The following list designates the sources of each question—that is, which question, task, or skill from each leading scholar that the item represents. You will see a great deal of overlap among sources. I have provided in italics an abbreviation for each, in the following:

- Brookfield's (2012b) Questions
    o Questions about the assumptions in an author's/researcher's work—*QAssump*
    o Questions about the evidence behind the validity of these assumptions—*QEvid*
    o Questions to generate alternative interpretations or explanations—*QAltern*
    o Questions to focus students on their own thinking—*QSelf-reg*
- Facione's (2020) Skills
    o Interpretation—*Interp*
    o Analysis—*Analyze*
    o Inference—*Infer*
    o Evaluation—*Eval*
    o Explanation—*Explain*
    o Deduction—*Deduce*
    o Induction—*Induce*
    o Numeracy—*Numer*
    o Self-regulation—*Self-reg*
- Halpern's (2014) Skills
    o Verbal reasoning—*VR*
    o Argument analysis—*AA*
    o Scientific reasoning—*SciR*
    o Statistical reasoning—*StatR*
    o Decision-making and problem-solving—*DM&PS*
- Elder and Paul's (2007; Paul & Elder, 2014) Universal Intellectual Standards
    o Clarity—*Clear*
    o Accuracy—*Accu*
    o Precision—*Prec*
    o Relevance—*Rel*
    o Significance—*Sign*
    o Completeness—*Compl*
    o Depth—*Depth*
    o Breadth—*Breadth*
    o Logic—*Logic*
    o Fairness—*Fair*

- Wolcott's (2006) Skills/Questions (grouped by step to better thinking)
  - Identifying problems, relevant information, and uncertainties—*ID*
  - Interpreting and analyzing arguments from multiple perspectives—*Interp & AA*
  - Analyzing and choosing among options—*A & Choose*
  - Tailoring communication to given audiences and settings—*Commun*
  - Being aware of shortcomings, seeking new information, and revising solutions—*Revise*

You may dispute a few of these source designations, but that shouldn't lessen the utility of this master list.

Synthesized Master List of 45 Critical Thinking Questions

1. What does this statement/claim/interpretation mean? What is a good way to understand it? *QAssump, Interp, VR, Clear, Interp & AA*
2. What led you to that interpretation? *QSelf-reg, Self-reg, Logic*
3. What is the best classification for this? *QAssump, Analyze, AA, Interp & AA*
4. What does the author(s) intend by this statement/claim? *QAssump, Infer, Interp & AA*
5. Would you classify this statement as a fact, an opinion, or an inference? Explain why. *QEvid, Explain, Analyze, AA, Logic*
6. What are the similarities and differences between/among these concepts/claims/conclusions? *QAssump, Analyze, AA, Prec, A & Choose*
7. What would you identify as the main hypothesis of this study? *QAssump, Analyze, SciR, Sign, ID*
8. How plausible is the claim made here? *QEvid, Eval, VR, AA, Accu, Interp & AA*
9. How much confidence can we put in the person who made it? *QAssump, Eval, VR*
10. How sound are the claims/arguments? What counterarguments/counterclaims can you offer? *QEvid, QAltern, Analyze, Eval, AA, Depth, Breadth, Logic, Interp & AA, A & Choose*
11. Can you identify any errors in reasoning (logical, statistical, scientific)? *QEvid, Analyze, Numer, AA, SciR, StatR, Accu, Rel, Sign, Compl, Logic, ID, Interp & AA*

12. How would you best state your claim/conclusion? *QAssump, AA, Clear, Prec, Commun*

13. What led you to this claim/conclusion? *QEvid, QSelf-reg, Explain, Self-reg, AA, SciR, StatR, Compl, A & Choose*

14. What assumptions lie behind your conclusion? *QAssump, Analyze, Explain, Deduce, AA, Interp & AA*

15. What if you assumed _____? How would your claim/conclusion change? *Altern, Infer, A & Choose*

16. If you accept this claim/conclusion, what are the consequences/ramifications? *Infer, AA, SciR, StatR*

17. Given the current facts, which claims/conclusions are valid? Which are ruled out? *QEvid, Eval, AA, SciR, StatR, Depth, Logic*

18. Does the evidence/data justify any other claims/conclusions? What are they? *QEvid, QAltern, Analyze, Infer, Deduce, AA, Breadth, Logic*

19. Given the current facts, how much confidence can we put in our claim/conclusion? *QEvid, SciR, StatR*

20. What are the implications of these data/information? Check your facts. *QEvid, Analyze, Infer, SciR, Accu, Prec, Compl, Logic, A & Choose*

21. What are the arguments on both sides? *QEvid, QAltern, Analyze, AA, Breadth, Logic, Interp & AA*

22. To resolve this issue/answer this question, what additional information/data do we need? *QEvid, Infer, Induce, AA, SciR, Compl, Revise*

23. What are some alternative explanations/conclusions/claims that we have not yet considered? *QAltern, Infer, AA, SciR, Compl, Revise*

24. What did this study/investigation/research find? *QAssump, Analyze, AA, SciR, Clear, Accu, Prec, ID*

25. How did you [or the author/researcher] conduct the study/investigation/research? *QEvid, AA, SciR, StatR, DM&PS, Logic, A & Choose*

26. How would you recount your reasoning on this issue? *QAssump, QSelf-reg, Explain, Self-reg, AA, Logic, Interp & AA*

27. What do you think was your best solution/answer? Why was it better than the alternative solutions/answers? *QEvid, Eval, DM&PS, Sign, Depth, A & Choose*

28. How solid is your evidence/data? *QEvid, Eval, SciR, Accu, Fair, Revise*

29. What evidence/data may be missing? *QEvid, Analyze, AA, Compl, Revise*

30. What additional evidence/data would benefit your study/research/argument? *QEvid, Analyze, AA, Compl, Revise*

31. These two conclusions seem to conflict. Do they really conflict? How might you reconcile them? *QAltern, Infer, AA, DM&PS, Logic, Interp & AA*

32. Which of these problems are most important to solve in terms of seriousness and urgency? *Analyze, DM&PS, Rel, Sign, Depth, A & Choose*

33. How likely is it that _____ will happen? How did you assess that likelihood? *Numer, StatR, Prec, Revise*

34. How does this new knowledge/finding relate to your prior knowledge? *QSelf-reg, Self-reg*

35. Is this problem like anything that you have encountered in the past? If so, can an analogy help you solve it? *QAltern, DM&PS, Breadth*

36. How can you recast your findings/conclusion as a graphic to communicate it better to you audience? *Commun*

37. How can you combine information/knowledge from different sources to forward a new claim/interpretation/conclusion? *QAltern, Induce*

38. What is the most important problem/issue? *QAssump, Analyze, AA, Rel, Sign, A & Choose*

39. What is the most suitable category for these observations/this information? *QAssump, Analyze, AA, Interp & AA*

40. Relationships between elements can be causal, sequential, spurious, or processual. What is the most suitable description for the relationship between elements here? *QEvid, Analyze, Numer, SciR, Accu, Prec, Depth, A & Choose*

41. How can you decide whether the relationship is causal or spurious? *QEvid, Analyze, Numer, SciR, Accu, Prec, Depth, A & Choose*

42. Can you recognize a pattern in the data? If so, what is it? *Infer, Induce, SciR, DM&PS*

43. These events could not have happened all at once. So in what order did they occur, and why? *Infer, SciR*

44. How do you know that your analysis/claim/conclusion is objective and impartial? Are you invested in it or any alternatives? *QSelf-reg, Self-reg, Fair, Revise*

45. What future trends or outcomes are most likely given the available evidence/information/data? *Infer, Deduce, Induce, SciR, StatR, Revise*

Whenever students answer a question or complete a task, they need feedback to know how well they performed. Otherwise, they may get practice in faulty thinking or not realize that their response is high-quality. The feedback may come from you, but it can also come from other students. In fact, when they appraise each other's contributions, students gain additional practice in critical thinking. Whether in a face-to-face or an online setting, invite the rest of the class to elaborate on, add to, complete, correct, or assess a peer's response. Allow students plenty of thinking time; don't underestimate the difficulty of the task. Two other sources of feedback online may be a computer program—at least for questions that have definite right answers—or a colleague that you bring into the discussion.

The Socratic Method: Spontaneous Questioning

Because we're on the topic of questions, let's delve into the Socratic method of questioning. Unlike the frameworks we've examined, it doesn't rely on a list of preconceived prompts. In fact, Socrates never described his method as "critical thinking" or any other kind of thinking. However, the Socratic method fosters modes of thought and dispositions that critical thinking requires, such as interpretation, analysis, reasoned thinking, pattern recognition, evaluation, self-examination, and persistence.

Here's how it works in a teaching context, including in law school, which relies heavily on this method. To open the dialogue, you ask the class a planned, course-relevant question that invites students to voice an opinion or take a stance on a given issue. One student ventures a response, and you spontaneously formulate a question that reveals an exception or a weakness in the student's answer. They then either defend or qualify their original response, or they assume a new position. You follow up with another question that serves the same purpose as the last one: to expose an exception to or weakness in the student's defense, qualified position, or new position. In turn, the student responds with a defense, a qualification, or another new position. The dialogue continues this way until . . . well, it's hard to say. Socrates could go on this way for hours. But in our world, it may end when the conversation raises an issue worth opening up to class discussion, when the student articulates a well-thought-out position, when the student "gives up," or when the bell rings.

The Socratic method presents serious challenges when applied in the face-to-face or online undergraduate classroom. The first pertains scalability because the method relies on a one-on-one conversation. What will other students be doing during this lengthy dialogue? You can make the Socratic method work only under these circumstances: (a) several students share the same viewpoint and you spread questions among them; (b) your students are willing and able to challenge each other with Socratic questions; or (c) you are tutoring a student privately. The second challenge to using the Socratic method is your ability to think of appropriate questions quickly, on the spot, in response to a student's position. You can't prepare, but experience can acquaint you with the unfounded generalizations and oversimplifications that students may voice on given issues. Finally, the Socratic method can come off as fault-finding, callous, and punitive. In law schools, it prepares students for adversarial situations. But in other classes, students don't expect to be pounded with questions that undermine their point. It can generate unnecessary stress and inhibit discussion. If you decide to experiment with the method, keep the class mood light and cheerful.

For more advice on using the Socratic method, you can access the Foundation for Critical Thinking (2019a, 2019b), if you are willing and able to pay for membership in the Critical Thinking Community.

Conclusion

If you are feeling a bit overwhelmed about meeting the challenge of teaching critical thinking, you need not. As with all new teaching methods, it's best to start small.

Before you start posing critical thinking prompts, examine the questions you already ask your students. Perhaps some of them do require critical thinking, but you haven't identified them as what they are. Then add a few critical thinking questions from this chapter's "master list" (pp. 71–73, this volume) perhaps to follow up on student responses during discussion or as short written reflections on a reading, lecture, video, or podcast. You will also find these questions useful in framing and debriefing debates, cases, simulations, and role-plays, which rank among the most effective methods for teaching critical thinking. Chapter 7 describes all such methods along with the most appropriate questions to pose to students.

7

USING THE MOST
EFFECTIVE METHODS
TO TEACH CRITICAL
THINKING

G iving your students active learning experiences is essential in teaching critical thinking (Burbach et al., 2004), but some active learning methods have proven to offer more effective practice than others in developing critical thinking skills. The literature includes some helpful empirical studies. In one study on business students (Braun, 2004), class discussion, debate, and guided questioning seemed to work especially well. In another on physics, Brookes and Lin (2010) cite whole-class discussion as giving the most effective practice in applying the epistemic principles of physics, which they argue to be equivalent to critical thinking. In a cross-disciplinary study, Edwards (2017) identifies class discussion, in-class critical thinking questioning, and reflective assignments as particularly valuable, with in-class questioning having the strongest impact. A meta-analysis by Abrami et al. (2014) presents perhaps the most compelling evidence favoring discussion based on instructor questions and applied problem-solving such as case studies, similations, games, and role-plays. It also highly recommends debate as a type of discussion. The article concludes:

> Two general types of instructional interventions are especially helpful in the development of generic CT [critical thinking] skills. Notably, the opportunity for dialogue (e.g., discussion) appears to improve the outcomes of CT skills acquisition, especially where the teacher poses questions, when there are both whole-class teacher-led discussions and teacher-led group discussions. Similarly, the exposure of students to authentic or situated

problems and examples seems to play an important role in promoting CT, particularly when applied problem-solving and role-playing methods are used. (p. 302)

We have already examined the most appropriate questions for an instructor to ask. Therefore, we can now consider ways to implement each effective major method. The critical thinking questions and tasks listed in the previous chapter will prove useful tools in all these methods.

Class Discussions

Class discussions can take place face-to-face or online; involve the entire class or student groups; and focus on essays, articles, books, arguments, assignments, examples, data, cases, and reflections, among other possible objects. Centering those discussions on critical thinking questions and tasks is key to developing your students' critical thinking skills.

Good discussions, including those in response to challenging questions, do not run themselves; you do, and you may benefit from some evidence-based guidance. As mentioned in chapter 3, you can obtain this guidance from any of several books that suggest ways to increase student participation (in class and online) and stimulate their high-level thinking (e.g., Brookfield & Preskill, 2005, 2016; Herman & Nilson, 2018; Howard, 2015). The appendix in this book includes strategies from Herman and Nilson (2018) to motivate students to prepare for discussion, listen actively during discussion, and contribute to a discussion.

Some basic advice is in order here. You want to be organized, look organized, and lead the discussion to a worthwhile destination, so start with planning. First, articulate that destination to yourself: What critical thinking questions or tasks do you want your students to be able to answer or perform to your satisfaction by the end of the discussion? These are your ultimate outcomes. Second, figure out what critical thinking questions or tasks that your students have to be able to answer or perform to your satisfaction before they can achieve your ultimate outcomes. Working backward like this is the same strategy recommended to design a course (Anderson et al., 2001; Fink, 2013; Nilson, 2016b; Wiggins & McTighe, 2005). In general, the discussion opens with lower-level questions and tasks and works up to higher-level ones.

Third, share a general sketch of your plan with your students before launching the discussion. Give them an outline or road map that lists the topics they will address, the questions or tasks they will discuss, or your learning outcomes for them. This will help your students see the learning process you have planned, follow your organization, and take notes on the discussion.

Fortunately, almost all critical thinking questions are of the type that encourage student contributions—those with multiple respectable answers. This feature lessens students' fears of giving a wrong answer and invites the exchange of diverse points of view and opinions.

Brookfield (2012b) has used a simple discussion framework called exemplars and flaws. You first ask students individually to identify "exemplars" from your course—that is, the most successful, interesting, effective, elegant, insightful, admirable, convincing, predictive, or plausible theory, law, proof, explanation, reading, piece of literature, author, or assignment—and to justify their choice. Then you ask students to name the flaws—that is, the least successful, effective, interesting, convincing, and so on—and to furnish reasons for their choices. Given no clear right or wrong answers, students feel free to volunteer their opinions. Just ask them to justify their answers.

Debates

Debate comes highly recommended for teaching critical thinking by Braun (2004), Seesholtz and Polk (2009), and Abrami et al. (2014), who classify it under discussion. You may recall from chapter 5 that Seesholtz and Polk (2009) team-taught a course to model civil disagreement, encourage mutual understanding, and promote fair evaluations of competing viewpoints. The simplest format for a debate is a two-sided, evidence-based argument with one side for the affirmative and the other for the negative, plus rebuttals. Each side has the same time limit and, in a course, is typically represented by a team of two to four students.

A variation on the simple debate, "point-counterpoint" brings all students into the activity in a small-group format (Silberman, 1996). The issue for this kind of debate must have at least a few different positions, however, because you will assign each group a position to represent. The groups can conduct their research during class or as homework, and each one should meet online or during class to coordinate their arguments. Right before presentation time, have each group sequence its members in some way—for example, in the order of their birthdays during the year. Then you select one of the #1 students to open the debate by stating one argument in favor of the group's stance. You move on to the #1 students in each group to present an argument for its stance, then on to the #2 students, the #3 students, and so on until all the students give all the arguments. Finally, you lead a whole-class discussion or discussion board comparing and evaluating the various positions.

Another variation, the "change-your-mind debate" also involves all your students in forming and re-forming their opinions. In the face-to-face version, you designate opposite sides of the classroom as agreeing with the affirmative or agreeing with the negative and reserve the middle of the room for those who are uncertain, undecided, or neutral. Before and during the debate, students sit in the sector that represents their current position and move to different sectors in the room as the debate sways their viewpoint. In the online version, students identify their current position and any shifts in opinion they make. After the debate, you ask those who changed their mind to explain what argument(s) precipitated them to switch and those taking the uncertain/undecided/neutral stance to give their analysis of the debate, as they probably have the fairest and most impartial take on it.

A final and particularly powerful variation on debate is "structured controversy" (also called "academic controversy") (Johnson et al., 1991). In this classic cooperative learning activity, you set up groups of four students, select a two-sided issue, and assign one side to one pair in each group and the other side to the other pair. After they prepare their respective cases, the pairs debate each other. Then—and this is the most powerful aspect—you have them switch sides, prepare their cases, debate again, and finally try to reconcile or synthesize the opposing sides. This last stage provides an excellent occasion for an individual paper and a meaningful assessment of student learning.

Debate and its variations occasion many of the critical thinking questions on the synthesized master list. Some of the following apply more to preparing one's side of the case and others more to formulating the rebuttal.

- Would you classify this statement as a fact, an opinion, or an inference, and why? *QEvid, Explain, Analyze, AA, Logic*
- What are the similarities and differences between (or among) these concepts/claims/conclusions? *QAssump, Analyze, AA, Prec, A & Choose*
- How plausible is the claim made here? *QEvid, Eval, VR, AA, Accu, Interp & AA*
- How much confidence can we put in the person who made it? *QAssump, Eval, VR*
- How sound are the claims/arguments? What counterarguments/counterclaims can you offer? *QEvid, QAltern, Analyze, Eval, AA, Depth, Breadth, Logic, Interp & AA, A & Choose*
- Can you identify any errors in reasoning (logical, statistical, scientific)? *QEvid, Analyze, Numer, AA, SciR, StatR, Accu, Rel, Sign, Compl, Logic, ID, Interp & AA*
- Given the current facts, which claims/conclusions are valid? Which are ruled out? *QEvid, Eval, AA, SciR, StatR, Depth, Logic*

- Does the evidence/data justify any other claims/conclusions? What are they? *QAltern, Analyze, Infer, Deduce, AA, Breadth, Logic*
- What are the implications of these data/information? Check your facts. *QEvid, Analyze, Infer, SciR, Accu, Prec, Compl, Logic, A & Choose*
- What are the arguments on both sides? *QEvid, QAltern, Analyze, AA, Breadth, Logic, Interp & AA*
- To resolve this issue/answer this question, what additional information/data do we need? *QEvid, Infer, Induce, AA, SciR, Compl, Revise*
- What are some alternative explanations/conclusions/claims that we have not yet considered? *QAltern, Infer, AA, SciR, Compl, Revise*
- What did this study/investigation/research find? *QAssump, Analyze, AA, SciR, Clear, Accu, Prec, ID*
- What do you think is your best solution/answer? Why is it better than the alternative solutions/answers? *QEvid, Eval, DM&PS, Sign, Depth, A & Choose*
- How solid is your evidence/data? *QEvid, Eval, SciR, Accu, Fair, Revise*
- What evidence/data may be missing? *QEvid, Analyze, AA, Compl, Revise*
- What additional evidence/data would benefit your study/research/argument? *QEvid, Analyze, AA, Compl, Revise*
- These two conclusions seem to conflict. Do they really conflict? How might you reconcile them? *QAltern, Infer, AA, DM&PS, Logic, Interp & AA*
- How can you combine information/knowledge from various sources to forward a new claim/interpretation/conclusion? *QAltern, Induce*
- Can you recognize a pattern in the data? If so, what is it? *Infer, Induce, SciR, DM&PS*
- Relationships between the elements can be causal, sequential, spurious, or processual. What is the most suitable description for the relationship between elements here? *QEvid, Analyze, Numer, SciR, Accu, Prec, Depth, A & Choose*
- Can you explain why you believe that your analysis/claim/conclusion is objective and impartial? How invested are you in it or any alternative? *QSelf-reg, Self-reg, Fair, Revise*

The Case Method

In the case method, students use course content and skills to analyze and develop feasible solutions to problematic situations or dilemmas that characters face in real or realistic stories. You can use a search engine to find cases for just about every discipline, or you can create your own cases tailored to your course. While most cases are printed, you increasingly find them dramatized on video recordings or embedded in online learning objects.

The realism of a challenging case stems from not only the credibility of the situation but also the uncertainty and risks surrounding possible problem-solving approaches. The dualistic or confused fact-finder perspective that most students bring to a beginning course will fail to lead them to suitable solutions. Therefore, they will have to deal with ambiguity and unknowns as they make critical, informed judgments about possible approaches. In addition, students must practice far transfer in applying course material and critical thinking skills to the cases (Edwards, 2017).

Brookfield (2012b) also endorsed the case method, but he called it "scenario analysis" (p. 59) and emphasized decision-making to take action. (This emphasis reflects Halpern's [2014] critical thinking skills of decision-making and problem-solving.) He asked students these critical thinking questions: What assumptions (or claims) does the main character bring to the situation? Which ones can you check out by research? Which ones is the character forgetting? With which ones would the character disagree? Brookfield's questions echo these from the synthesized master list of critical thinking questions in the previous chapter: What do you think the author intends by this statement/claim? What did this study/investigation find? What are some alternative explanations/conclusions/claims that we have not yet considered?

Depending upon the case, good debriefing questions can take other directions, too—all of which reflect our synthesized master list of questions. Here are some that require interpretation or analysis: What is the main problem in this case? Whose problem is it? Why do you think that [specific character] did [action]? Why do you think that [specific character] did not take action? What were the consequences of this action (or inaction)? What role do you think the context played? (The context may be the organizational or national culture, financial limitations, the historical period, or something else.) If the context were different (another culture, time, place, financial situation, etc.), would the situation play out another way? How would the problem morph?

After analyzing the problem, lead students into evaluative questions about how this problematic situation could be resolved and perhaps prevented. Which course concepts and principles would elucidate answers? What are some possible solutions or preventions? What are the most relevant criteria for assessing the alternatives (e.g., feasibility, comprehensiveness, cost, effort, trade offs, etc.). Applying the key criteria, which option is best, and why?

Simulations, Games, and Role-Plays

Simulations and academically useful games abound, especially for business and the social sciences. In these experiential activities, students play roles without a script in problematic interpersonal or social situations that contain conflict, uncertainty, or both. In simulations, the situations imitate important aspects of real life that are usually discipline-related, while games are more abstract and not necessarily discipline-relevant. For example, when students play Jeopardy or Who Wants to Be a Millionaire? to review factual material for a test, the questions come from the course material, but the game is unrelated to it.

You can find available simulations the same way you can cases: Put a topic of interest and the word "simulations" into a search engine. (Nilson [2016b] also furnishes URLs to locate some simulations and games.) Most options are now played online. Unlike most cases, however, simulations and games do not come free. Harvard Business School cases also cost money.

Brookfield's (2012a) Crisis Decision Simulation illustrates a gray area between simulations and games. Facing time limitations, urgency, and uncertainty, a group of participants must make life-and-death decisions about who can and cannot get into a lifeboat. The challenge is abstract, as with a game, in that the activity has no specific connection to a discipline.

Two well-known supply-chain simulations call themselves games: the Supply Chain Game and the Beer Game. But both are serious, competitive simulations that demonstrate the challenges of being a part of a supply network—suppliers, manufacturers, salespeople, and customers—and the need to coordinate. Each team of students can control only one segment of the chain. But if the team orders too much or too little, the imbalance impacts every segment of the chain, and the decisions that each team makes affect the decisions of others. Students arrive at decisions about control parameters, logistics, transportation, expansions, and warehouses, all to try to maximize their cash position in the end. Along the way, they can learn how to forecast, control inventory and production, design a supply network, and avoid the common problems that arise from poor coordination. Both simulations can continue for a week or two.

Role-plays imitate reality but on a smaller, more interpersonal scale, so unlike simulations and games, they rarely involve the entire class as actors. Usually the players have different sets of information and sometimes conflicting goals. The most common contexts for role-plays are counseling, clinical psychology, nursing, and teaching, but management and the social sciences also use them to teach negotiation, mediation, conflict resolution, and bargaining.

All these experiential activities demand critical thinking. Not every question on the synthesis master list will apply, but the ones following do because they are often useful in making strategic decisions. Note how many critical thinking skills are identified:

- How would you best state your claim/conclusion? *QAssump, AA, Clear, Prec, Commun*
- What led you to this claim/conclusion? *QEvid, QSelf-reg, Explain, Self-reg, AA, SciR, StatR, Compl, A & Choose*
- What assumptions lie behind your claim/conclusion? *QAssump, Analyze, Explain, Deduce, AA, Interp & AA*
- What if you assumed _____? How would your claim/conclusion change? *Altern, Infer, A & Choose*
- If you accept this claim/conclusion, what are the consequences/ramifications? *Infer, AA, SciR, StatR*
- Given the current facts, which claims/conclusions are valid? Which are ruled out? *QEvid, Eval, AA, SciR, StatR, Depth, Logic*
- Does the evidence/data justify any other claims/conclusions? What are they? *QAltern, Analyze, Infer, Deduce, AA, Breadth, Logic*
- Given the current facts, how much confidence can we put in our claim/conclusion? *QEvid, SciR, StatR,*
- What are the implications of these data/information? Check your facts. *QEvid, Analyze, Infer, SciR, Accu, Prec, Compl, Logic, A & Choose*
- What are the arguments on both sides? *QEvid, QAltern, Analyze, AA, Breadth, Logic, Interp & AA*
- To resolve this issue/answer this question, what additional information/data do we need? *QEvid, Infer, Induce, AA, SciR, Compl, Revise*
- What are some alternative explanations/conclusions/claims that we have not yet considered? *QAltern, Infer, AA, SciR, Compl, Revise*
- What do you think is your best solution/answer? Why is it better than the alternative solutions/answers? *QEvid, Eval, DM&PS, Sign, Depth, A & Choose*
- How solid is your evidence? *QEvid, Eval, SciR, Accu, Fair, Revise*
- What evidence/data might be missing? *QEvid, Analyze, AA, Compl, Revise*
- What additional evidence/data would benefit your study/research/argument? *QEvid, Analyze, AA, Compl, Revise*
- These two conclusions seem to conflict. Do they really conflict? How might you reconcile them? *QAltern, Infer, AA, DM&PS, Logic, Interp & AA*

- Which of these problems are more important to solve in terms of seriousness and urgency? *Analyze, DM&PS, Rel, Sign, Depth, A & Choose*
- How likely is it that _____ will happen? How did you assess that likelihood? *Numer, StatR, Prec, Revise*
- How does this new knowledge/finding relate to your prior knowledge? *QSelf-reg, Self-reg*
- These events could not have happened all at once. So in what order did they occur, and why? *Infer, SciR*
- How do you know that your analysis/claim/conclusion is objective and impartial? Are you invested in it or any alternative? *QSelf-reg, Self-reg, Fair, Revise*
- What future trends or outcomes are most likely given the available evidence/information/data? *Infer, Deduce, Induce, SciR, StatR, Revise*

Advancing Students' Critical Thinking Skills Through Your Course

Of course, you want your students to improve their critical thinking skills during your course. You can choose either of the following strategies to do so, or a combination of the two. First, you can assign students increasingly complex material to interpret, analyze, and evaluate over time. In other words, you can pose essentially the same critical thinking questions on progressively more challenging reading, video, or podcast assignments. Second, you can move your students through a stage model. In chapter 2, we summarized three of them:

- Perry's (1968) four-stage theory of undergraduate cognitive development, which focuses on students' understanding of the nature of knowledge (epistemology);
- Wolcott's (2006) five-step model of better thinking, which applies best to decision-making; and
- Elder and Paul's (2010) six-stage developmental model of critical thinking maturity, which centers on metacognition and self-regulated learning.

Of course, you may be able to combine the two approaches—incorporating increasingly complex material through the steps or phases of a stage model.

If you decide to implement the first or a combination strategy, you might start by ordering your reading (or video or podcast) assignments from the least to the most complex. If you prefer the second or a combination strategy, select the stage model most compatible with your subject matter and learning outcomes and then order your reading assignments by complexity. Do visit the original source for more detail on helping students progress from stage to stage. In addition, you might choose the specific questions from the synthetized master list that you will ask your students in discussion or as a writing assignment while you guide them through the stages.

Conclusion

You may already be using teaching methods in your courses that can build your students' critical thinking skills. Do you have discussions, debates, cases, simulations, games, or role-plays in any of your courses? In addition to fostering critical thinking, these methods serve a variety of higher-level learning outcomes very well and merit consideration in any course. Discussions and cases are particularly easy to add, and students enjoy them if well managed. Large class size need not discourage you because most of these methods adapt seamlessly to small-group work.

If your courses rely very little or not at all on these methods, consider trying out one or two of them in one course and assessing their effects on student learning. Sometimes a method that doesn't work well the first time deserves another trial in a later course offering after you collect student feedback or learn more about implementing the method.

When you plan discussions, debates, cases, simulations, games, or role-plays, incorporate the types of questions that chapter 6 recommends—those that require your students to practice critical thinking skills. There is little point in using a method to teach these skills if the questions or debriefing sessions do not demand critical thinking.

Because you may be among the many instructors who design their courses to move students through increasingly complex and challenging material, you may have already structured your courses to advance your students' critical thinking skills. For now, reserve the stage models for the next time you develop a new course.

8

ASSESSING YOUR STUDENTS' CRITICAL THINKING WITH OBJECTIVE ITEMS

L et's open this first of four chapters on assessment with some observations about the topic in general and the assessment of critical thinking specifically.

How successful have your students been in achieving your learning outcomes for them? Assessments, whether formal (graded) or informal (ungraded or low-stakes), answer this crucial question. Your informal (also called formative) assessments should provide your students with practice in your outcomes as well as whatever steps they need to take before attempting your outcomes for a grade. This practice can help ensure that your students perform well on your formal (also called summative) assessments. The most effective teaching methods furnish this practice. Formative assessments also give you valuable feedback on your students' learning progress. How else will you know whether to provide them with additional clarification, modeling, and practice or move along to the next topic? While your students will progress at different speeds, try to ensure that at least 80% of them perform adequately before moving on.

In chapter 4, we considered the scientific abilities developed by the Rutgers Physics and Astronomy Education (2014) group for a calculus-based, lab-oriented, undergraduate-level physics course (see also Etkina et al., 2006):

- Design and conduct an observational experiment, including deciding what variables to measure and how to measure them.
- Design and conduct a testing experiment, including deciding what variables to measure and how to measure them.

- Design and conduct an application experiment, including deciding what variables to measure and how to measure them.
- Gather and analyze experimental data.
- Represent information, data, or findings in multiple ways.
- Evaluate equations, solutions, models, and claims.
- Communicate scientific ideas clearly.

We included these in the comprehensive list of learning outcomes/skills for the sciences.

Brookes and Lin (2010) also integrated the abilities (and subabilities) in their introductory physics course as the criteria in formative assessment rubrics. The instructors used the rubrics to not only provide their students with feedback but also help them focus their learning and acquire practice in evaluating their own work. Before finishing the course, the students showed learning gains comparable to those achieved by interactive methods.

As we turn to summative assessment, you may think that you can evaluate critical thinking skills only with an essay exam, a report write-up, or a paper assignment, but this isn't true. For most critical thinking skills, you can use either "selected-response" assessments, better known as objective items, or what are called "constructed-response" assessments like essays, papers, and projects. This chapter address the former type. Chapter 9 considers how to design prompts for the latter type. In addition, you have two options for assessing and grading your students' constructed responses: rubrics, which work well in a point-based system, or specifications grading, which assess on a pass/fail basis. Chapters 10 and 11 explain each option, respectively.

Now, let's look at strategies for assessing your students' critical thinking skills with objective items.

Types of Objective Items

You can compose most types of objective items—matching, multiple-choice, true/false, and multiple true/false—to require and assess these high-level critical thinking skills:

- interpretation
- generalization
- inference
- deduction
- induction
- problem-solving

- decision-making
- conclusion drawing
- analysis
- evaluation
- numeracy

In fact, the only kind of objective item that you can't design to assess critical thinking is the completion or fill-in-the-blank item, which can test only memorization or one-precise-right-answer questions. Given this limitation, it is especially well-suited to testing mathematical problem-solving and foreign language writing at the language acquisition level (if the French word *enchanté* is missing the accent *aigu* over the second "e," the spelling is wrong). In other disciplines, spelling and strict precision may be less important.

Writing Matching Items to Assess Critical Thinking

In a matching test, students search for the answer to or complement of the items on the left side among the items on the right side. Theoretically, every option in the right column is a plausible match for every item in the left column. Standard matching tests typically require only recognition of basic knowledge. Common tasks involve matching each theory (on the left) with its originator (on the right), each cause with its effect, each definition with a term (or vice versa), each symbol with a concept, each achievement or work with its person or author, each foreign word with its translation, each picture of an object with its name, each biological organ (its name or a picture of it) with its purpose, or each piece of equipment or apparatus with its use or function.

We think of only one item on the right pairing correctly with one item on the left, but this need not be the case. To add challenge, you can specify that an item on the right may be used more than once or not at all. Or you can allow an item on the left to have two or more correct matches on the right, and the student must identify both or all to give a correct answer. Or you can name a process, procedure, or sequence of events on the left and have items on the right that comprise parts of the process, procedure, or sequence. Of course, a student must put the parts in the correct order.

However difficult the task may be for students, it does not entail critical thinking if they have seen the pairings before. Still, you can assess critical thinking by writing items for the left or the right column that they haven't seen before, such as familiar concepts on the left with new examples of them on the right, or new problems on the left with the tools, approaches, or algorithms needed to solve them on the right.

If you decide to write such a matching test, think first about what two sets of items you can have your students match that assess their critical thinking skills. Be sure each set is grammatically parallel (all sentences, all gerunds, all nouns, etc.) and restrict the number of items to whatever will fit on one page or one screen.

Writing Multiple-Choice and Multiple True–False Items to Assess Critical Thinking

You might take some time to complete the sample items from the California Critical Thinking Skills Test (Insight Assessment, 2013b). Note that a scenario or stimulus precedes each multiple-choice item or set of such items. Now reflect: While you were answering these sample items, what critical thinking skills were you aware of using?

No doubt you have seen one or a series of multiple-choice items that required you to interpret, analyze, and evaluate a scenario or stimulus before. Recall the standardized tests you took before college, graduate school, or professional school: the SAT Reasoning Test, the Graduate Record Exam (GRE), the Graduate Management Admissions Test (GMAT), or the Medical College Admissions Test (MCAT). Professional test designers and assessment experts develop these items for the purpose of evaluating reasoning skills, to include critical thinking. This type of multiple-choice item is called "stimulus based." It is one multiple-choice item or a series of them that require students to correctly interpret or analyze a new (to the students), realistic stimulus. Writing a series of items around one stimulus maximizes efficiency.

Stimuli come in the following kinds, none of which you are likely to find in a publisher's test bank:

- Text—for example, a claim, quote, statement, report, passage, word problem, short case, text-based data set, or description of a research study or research results
- Graphics—for example, a graph, table, chart, diagram, model, map, picture, drawing, spreadsheet, or schematic
- Audio recordings—for example, music, speeches, radio broadcasts, or podcasts
- Videos or animations—for example, a dramatized case, scenario, story, or situation or a simulation of a process, procedure, or sequence of events

While students should not have seen the specific stimulus before, they should have had the opportunity to practice interpreting or analyzing that kind of stimulus before getting summatively assessed on the skill. In addition, they should not have to contend with too many, if any, interlocking items in a series of items around one stimulus. Interlocking means that getting one item correct depends on getting one or more other items correct.

Whatever kind of multiple-choice items you write, all the options should be plausible, grammatically parallel, about the same length, and listed in some way that doesn't hint at the correct answer (alphabetically, chronologically, numerically, or randomly). If you have trouble coming up with distracters (wrong answers), try creating them from the elements of the correct response—that is, the variables, people, events, and so on in that response. Massa and Kasimatis (2017), Parkes and Zimmaro (2016), and Sibley (2014) offer guidance on constructing good multiple-choice and other types of selected-response items.

Let's look at a few examples of stimulus-based multiple-choice items developed around the data in a table (see Table 8.1). Every set of these items should assess at least one of your course learning outcomes. The three items following assess students' ability to interpret tabular data.

The following three multiple-choice items are related to the data in Table 8.1. Pick the one correct answer for each item.

1. The table shows:
   a. the mean value of the debt held by U.S. households by type of debt and selected characteristics in 2016.
   b. the median value of the debt held by U.S. households by selected characteristics and type of debt, 2016.*
   c. the relationship between annual household income and household net worth by selected characteristics, 2016.
   d. the mean secured and unsecured household debt of U.S. householders of different races and Hispanic origin, 2016.
   e. none of the above
2. The table does *not* show:
   a. the relationship between householder race or Hispanic origin and the median value of household debt, 2016.
   b. the relationship between annual household income and the median value of secured household debt, 2016.
   c. the relationship between household net worth and the median value of unsecured household debt, 2016.
   d. the relationship between annual household income and household net worth, 2016.*
   e. the relationship between age of householder and the median value of total debt, 2016.

TABLE 8.1
Median Value of Debt for U.S. Households, by Type of Debt and Selected Characteristics: 2016

Characteristic	Total Debt ($)	Secured Debt				Unsecured Debt			
		Total ($)	Home Debt ($)	Business Debt ($)	Vehicle Debt ($)	Total ($)	Credit Card Debt ($)	Student Loans ($)	Other Debt ($)
Total	61,060	87,000	123,000	20,000	13,000	8,000	3,500	20,000	3,000
Race and Hispanic Origin of Householder									
White alone	66,600	90,350	120,000	20,000	13,270	8,000	3,500	20,000	3,000
White not Hispanic	72,600	95,000	120,000	22,500	14,000	8,000	3,900	20,000	3,500
Black alone	34,500	41,000	107,000	(B)	13,000	8,000	3,000	20,000	2,700
Asian alone	107,000	170,000	240,000	(B)	14,400	6,000	4,000	15,000	3,000
Other (residual)	42,000	50,000	126,900	(B)	11,000	10,000	3,000	19,060	4,000
Hispanic origin (any race)	36,000	66,120	135,000	5,810	12,000	6,000	3,000	16,220	2,400
Age of Householder									
Less than 35 years	42,000	53,000	140,000	20,000	12,000	12,000	2,400	20,000	3,450
35 to 44 years	97,400	115,000	150,000	20,000	15,000	10,000	4,000	22,000	3,500
45 to 54 years	91,800	108,300	130,000	20,000	14,000	9,000	5,000	18,000	3,400
55 to 64 years	61,000	84,010	103,300	20,000	14,000	6,000	4,000	17,000	3,000
65 to 69 years	43,500	70,000	92,000	(B)	12,000	5,000	3,800	13,000	3,000
70 to 74 years	34,690	64,770	90,000	(B)	12,000	4,000	3,000	13,000	3,000
75 and over	16,760	49,420	75,000	(B)	11,000	2,500	2,000	9,000	2,380

(Continues)

TABLE 8.1 (Continued)

Characteristic	Total Debt ($)	Secured Debt				Unsecured Debt			
		Total ($)	Home Debt ($)	Business Debt ($)	Vehicle Debt ($)	Total ($)	Credit Card Debt ($)	Student Loans ($)	Other Debt ($)
Annual Household Income									
Lowest quintile	13,100	23,610	75,000	10,000	8,000	4,350	2,000	14,500	2,700
Second quintile	20,400	30,000	80,000	10,000	10,000	5,000	2,000	15,000	3,000
Third quintile	47,280	60,000	97,000	15,300	12,000	6,020	3,000	20,000	2,500
Fourth quintile	99,000	99,360	120,000	25,000	14,000	10,600	4,500	21,000	3,652
Highest quintile	185,900	187,500	197,000	31,500	18,000	14,000	5,700	23,000	6,000
Household Net Worth									
Negative or zero	35,600	20,000	123,000	(B)	12,010	23,200	4,000	36,000	5,000
$1 to $4,999	4,000	10,000	74,260	(B)	8,000	1,650	1,100	8,000	1,000
$5,000 to $9,999	7,000	14,000	88,000	(B)	7,311	3,500	1,900	10,000	2,300
$10,000 to $24,999	22,000	30,000	90,000	(B)	10,700	6,165	3,000	15,000	2,500
$25,000 to $49,999	49,100	69,000	88,140	(B)	12,000	5,500	3,000	12,000	2,810
$50,000 to $99,999	74,600	90,000	107,800	(B)	12,200	5,822	3,000	15,000	3,000
$100,000 to $249,999	86,000	100,000	116,000	14,000	15,000	7,000	4,000	18,000	3,000
$250,000 to $499,999	93,600	113,000	130,000	14,000	15,000	5,700	3,900	14,000	2,500
$500,000 and over	152,400	180,000	178,600	60,000	16,000	7,000	4,000	15,000	5,000

Note: (B)—Base is less than 200,000 households, or sample size less than 50. Estimates rounded to four significant digits.

Source: U.S. Census Bureau, Survey of Income and Program Participation, 2014 Panel,

Wave 4 at https://www.census.gov/data/tables/2016/demo/wealth/wealth-asset-ownership.html

Internet Release Date: 9/25/2019

3. The data in the table suggest that in 2016:
   a. households of higher annual income held a higher median value of debt than households of lower annual income.*
   b. Asian-led households carried less total debt than the households led by members of other racial and ethnic groups.
   c. households in the lowest quintile of annual income held more total debt than households in the higher quintiles.
   d. the median value of household student loan debt declined as annual household income increased.
   e. all of the above

(* designates the correct answer.)

Stimulus-based true/false items can also assess critical thinking skills. In fact, determining true from false statements is the foundation of multiple true-false items. In this lesser-known type of objective item, each option following the stem is a true/false item, and the number of options may vary from four to 10. You will probably find these items easier to compose than multiple-choice items, and students find them more challenging because they cannot rely on the process of elimination. (If you wish, you can provide the number of the statements that are true to make the task a little easier for students.) Furthermore, these items offer greater efficiency and reliability. One multiple-choice item with five options presents students with just one decision point, while the same stem with five multiple true/false options gives students five decision points, therefore increasing the reliability of the test results.

While the stem must be clear, this is easy to ensure. You can always use this standard stem: "Given the quote (or claim, short case, description, data in the table, study results, graph, diagram, etc.) above (or on the screen), which of the following statements is/are true?"

For example, here is a set of multiple true/false items that, like the multiple-choice items before, assess students' ability to interpret tabular data.

The following six items are multiple true/false. Given the data in Table 8.1, which of the following statements is/are true? Mark T for true and F for false next to the item.

_____1. The median value of secured and unsecured household debt varies directly with annual household income.*
_____2. In households that have a positive net worth, the median value of secured debt varies directly with household net worth.*
_____3. The median value of total secured household debt varies negatively with age of the householder.

_____4. The highest median value of household credit card debt is held by householders who are younger than 35 years old.

_____5. Compared to households led by Asians (alone), households led by Blacks (alone) hold a higher median home debt.

_____6. Households with a negative or zero net worth hold more unsecured debt than any other net-worth group of households.*

(* designates true statements.)

The stimulus for the next example is a description of a double experiment in cognitive psychology (McDaniel et al., 2009), and the set of multiple true/false items after it assesses students' ability to interpret and analyze the abstracted results of an experimental research study:

> The study involved two experiments, using college students as subjects, designed to test the effectiveness of a learning strategy called the 3Rs (read-recite-review). In this strategy, the learner first reads the material, then free-recalls as much of it as possible, then reviews the material for missed or misunderstood ideas. Three groups of subjects received the same amount of time to study the same academic material. One group used the 3R strategy, the second group rereading, and the third group note-taking. Immediately after and again 1 week later, the subjects were tested on the material using free-recall, multiple-choice, and short-answer inference items. The only difference in the second experiment was the reading material; it was longer, more complex, and more technical (on engineering topics). In the first experiment, the 3R group significantly outperformed the other two groups in both immediate and delayed free recall of fact-based passages. In the second experiment, the 3R group outperformed the rereading group on multiple-choice and problem-solving items and performed as well as the note-taking group.

The following seven items are multiple true/false. Given the description of the preceding experiment, which of the following statements is/are true? Mark T for true and F for false next to the item.

_____1. In both experiments, the subjects in the note-taking group scored higher on all three of the tests than the subjects in the other two groups.

_____2. In the second experiment, the subjects in the 3R group required more time to complete their studying than did subjects in the other two groups.

_____3. In both experiments, how well the subjects in the rereading group performed on the tests depended on how many times they reread the material.

____4. The results of both experiments show that the 3R strategy is consistently more effective than the rereading strategy.*

____5. The results of the second experiment show that the 3R strategy is consistently more effective than the note-taking strategy.

____6. The second experiment found that subjects in the 3R and the note-taking groups performed equally well on the multiple-choice and problem-solving items.*

____7. Both experiments together show that all three of the learning strategies tested are equally effective.

(* designates true statements.)

As with multiple-choice items, all the options should be plausible, grammatically parallel, about the same length, and listed in some way that doesn't cue the correct answer. You can always create distracters using the elements of the correct response(s).

Conclusion

Using objective items, you can assess your students' critical thinking with a matching test involving one column that your students haven't seen before or with stimulus-based multiple-choice, true/false, or multiple true-false objective items. The challenge for the latter type of item is finding an appropriate stimulus and writing a series of relevant items around the stimulus.

What kinds of stimuli (text, graphic, audio, video, or animation) would be appropriate to use in your courses for objective items that can assess critical thinking skills? What kinds of stimuli does your discipline use? Passages from literature? Reports? Word problems? Cases? Experiments? Survey results? Tables? Graphs? Diagrams? Maps? Pictures? Schematics? Models? Spreadsheets? Audio recordings? Simulations? Where might you find such stimuli? Magazines? Academic journals? News reports? Textbooks you're not using for your courses? An internet archive (e.g., The Internet Archive at https://archive.org/web/) or educational repository (e.g., MERLOT at https://www.merlot.org/ or WISC-Online at http://www.wisc-online.com/)? If you are looking for such stimuli, they often appear unexpectedly.

Once you find a good stimulus, review and follow the best practices previously discussed (e.g., all the options should be plausible, grammatically parallel, about the same length, etc.) in drafting a series of items that require one or more of your students' critical thinking skills. This is a creative endeavor that may prove more energizing and enjoyable than you expect.

Objective items can assess critical thinking skills more efficiently than constructed-response questions and tasks, but they cannot assess students' achievement on all possible critical thinking learning outcomes. In particular, they cannot assess students' abilities to create, communicate, define problems, design something, organize, or conduct research. For such outcomes, only constructed responses can, and chapter 9 addresses how best to design the prompts.

9

ASSESSING YOUR STUDENTS' CRITICAL THINKING WITH CONSTRUCTED-RESPONSE QUESTIONS AND TASKS

O bjective items may not be able to assess all the critical thinking skills you have in mind for your course—for instance, your students' abilities to create, communicate, define problems, design something, organize, or conduct research. Though not as efficient as objective items, constructed-response questions and tasks can assess *any* critical thinking skill.

Constructed responses can take on many forms: writing assignments, essay test questions, live oral presentations, multimedia presentations, computer programs, projects, research reports, designs (graphic, engineering, architectural, landscape), artistic works or performances, portfolios— really any product that students create. A well-designed constructed-response prompt may have multiple respectable responses, just like a good discussion prompt. In addition, the task is well-defined—that is, students should be able to discern exactly what you're asking them to do. If you have concerns about how they may interpret the prompt, then by all means provide hints about the content or types of thinking you would like them to use. With challenging questions and tasks, such hints lend fair and often needed help.

To assess critical thinking, a good constructed-response prompt also has something in common with a good objective item: a stimulus. For the former, it is often a realistic problem, paradox, puzzle, or disquieting situation, whether expressed in text, a graphic, an audio file, a video, or an animation. For example, look back at Table 8.1. Median Value of Debt for Households, by Type of Debt and Selected Characteristics: 2016 (pp. 91–92, this volume). Here is one possible constructed-response question (actually two questions) that presents students with a puzzle related to that table.

Refer to the data in the table, Median Value of Debt for Households, by Type of Debt and Selected Characteristics: 2016, to develop your answer to this essay question. Which three or four groups of U.S. households have the worst debt problem, and how did you determine these groups?

Reminder: The true burden of a household's debt is relative to that household's income and wealth. In addition, be aware that secured debt is less burdensome than unsecured debt. Let's take a household holding secured debts of $200,000 and unsecured debts of $20,000 with an annual income in the highest quintile and a net worth of $1 million. This is a total debt value of $220,000. Let's take another household holding secured debts of $30,000 and unsecured debt of $10,000 with an annual income in the lowest quintile and a net worth of $15,000. This is a total debt value of $40,000. Which household is more burdened by debt? The second household is, because, compared to the former household, its debts are relatively larger than its annual income and net worth. In addition, the second household has relatively more unsecured debt, even though it is half of what the former holds.

Keep these economic complexities in mind as you consider the debt problems of various groups and justify your determination of the most debt-burdened.

To answer these questions, students must not only interpret the data in the table correctly but also analyze the data from different columns and rows to uncover the implications of various socioeconomic statuses for Americans.

You can mine good constructed-response prompts from your critical thinking learning outcomes by turning them into questions and tasks that you situate in the subject-matter context of your course. Chapter 6 (p. 62, this volume) gave examples on how to do this for teaching critical thinking skills, specifically for developing questions to ask your students in discussion and low-stakes writing assignments. This strategy helps ensure that you assess your students' achievement of your outcomes as directly as possible. The critical thinking questions on our synthesized master list also make excellent constructed-response prompts when connected to an appropriate stimulus, such as a complex case, problem, simulation, game, or role-play. Whatever critical thinking questions you have used in teaching constitute reasonable assessment prompts. Your students should be well prepared to respond to them.

You may have written some essay questions or assignment directions in the past that you may want to upgrade to incorporate critical thinking. Here are some examples of such upgraded prompts focused around a realistic problem, paradox, or disquieting situation (Nilson, 2016a, Unit 4.1; reprinted with permission from Magna Publications):

Low-level and ill-defined: To what factors have historians attributed the decline of the Roman Empire?

Upgraded: Some people argue that the United States is following the same path of decline as the Roman Empire. Write a critical examination of this claim analyzing how the United States is and is not declining due to similar factors.

Low-level and ill-defined: What should a nurse do when a patient has a bad reaction to an immunotherapy injection?

Upgraded: After the first injection of an immunotherapy program, you notice a large, red wheal on your patient's arm. Then the patient begins coughing and expiratory wheezing. What series of interventions should you implement? Justify your interventions and their sequence.

Low-level and ill-defined: What is the relationship between education and income? To what extent has it changed recently?

Upgraded: The education of the working and middle classes has been increasing for several decades while their income has been flat or decreasing for the past two decades. How can you resolve this trend with the well-established positive relationship between education and income? (Consider other factors that may affect income.)

Low-level and ill-defined: What will happen to the hydrosphere, the geosphere, and the biosphere if a large amount of sulfur dioxide is released into the atmosphere?

Upgraded: Some geoscientists maintain that the mega-magna chamber below Yellowstone National Park is leaking increasing amounts of sulfur dioxide into the atmosphere and will cause a mass extinction within 70,000 years. They rest this claim on the mass extinction that is believed to have happened 250 million years ago. Why or why not do you accept this claim? To what extent are the hydrospheric, atmospheric, and biospheric conditions comparable to those 250 million years ago?

In mathematics, physics, and physical chemistry, you can assess students' critical thinking skills with context-rich problems. These are relevant, challenging, and well-structured problems. Unlike traditional problems, they do not provide drawings, assumptions, or predefined variables. The University of Minnesota (UMN) developed many dozens of these problems for group and individual exams given in the algebra-based introductory physics courses and the calculus-based courses. Many of them address topics in mechanics, including linear kinematics, forces and acceleration, forces and circular motion at a constant speed, conservation of energy, conservation of momentum, rotational kinematics and dynamics, and oscillations and waves. Others pertain to electromagnetism, specifically electrical field and electrical force, electric potential energy, electric power, circuits, and magnetic field and force, among other topics. They are all available in the UMN Physics' problem archive (University of Minnesota, 2012), along with guidelines on how to develop your own context-rich problems. Here is one of these problems as an illustration:

> You read in the newspaper that rocks from Mars have been found on Earth. Your friend says that the rocks were shot off Mars by the large volcanoes there. You are skeptical, so you decide to calculate the magnitude of the velocity that volcanoes eject rocks from the geological evidence. You know the gravitational acceleration of objects falling near the surface of Mars is only 40 percent that on the Earth. You assume that you can look up the height of Martian volcanoes and find some evidence of the distance that rocks from the volcano hit the ground from pictures of the Martian surface. If you assume that the rocks farthest from a volcano were ejected at an angle of 45 degrees, what is the magnitude of the rock's velocity as a function of its distance from the volcano and the height of the volcano for the rock farthest from the volcano? [Explain your reasoning through your process of solving this problem.](University of Minnesota, 2012, "Two-dimensional motion at a constant acceleration (projectile)" section, para. 12)

The final sentence (bracketed) was added to enhance the critical thinking value of the problem and incorporate self-regulated learning.

Developing a Reflective Meta-Assignment/Assignment Wrapper

As emphasized in chapters 3 and 5, critical thinking demands explicit awareness, monitoring, control, and evaluation of one's thinking. Therefore, it is wise to add to each constructed-response assignment a meta-assignment or assignment wrapper in which students reflect on and describe their thinking and affective processes (Edwards, 2017; Facione, 2000). Even if student responses to these meta-assignments run a few pages, you can grade them pass/fail or credit/no credit by following the guidelines for specifications grading in chapter 11.

Papers and projects vary so much in their purpose and learning outcomes that the most appropriate reflection prompts may include any of those following. All the prompts are adapted from Nilson (2013):

- Describe how you arrived at your response/solution. What was your reasoning/research process?
- How did you define the task/problem? How did you determine which principles and concepts from the course to apply? How did you devise alternative approaches and solutions? On what grounds did you assess them to decide on the best alternative?
- How did you conduct your design/problem-solving/research process? What steps did you take? What strategies did you devise and follow? What problems did you encounter? How did you move beyond these problems? (With a problem-solving process reflection, students begin to abstract and adopt a more expert approach to complex problems.)
- Reflect on the value of this assignment. What knowledge did you gain? What skills did you develop or improve? When in the future do you think they will be useful to you?
- Did anything that you learned challenge your prior thoughts on the subject? If so, did you feel yourself resisting, and how did you overcome this feeling?
- Evaluate your strategies, performance, and success in achieving your goals. Given what you have learned, what would you do differently if you were going through this experience again?
- How would you assess your progress/improvement from previous similar assignments?
- For follow-up after receiving peer and instructor feedback: How would you paraphrase the written feedback you received on this product? What feedback did you find most useful? What feedback did you find least useful?
- For a group paper or project: How well do you think you worked with other group members on this paper/project? What problems did your group encounter? How did your group overcome them? What did you learn about group assignments from this experience?
- For a revision: What goals and strategies will guide your revision?
- For a portfolio: How would you evaluate your progress in your work through this course? In what areas of weakness did you improve, and what strengths did you develop or refine?
- In regard to this assignment, what advice would you give the next group of students taking this course? How would you advise these

students on how to prepare for the assignment, how to approach it, what challenges to expect, how to overcome them, and what value they may find in it?

In addition to some of the preceding questions, those that follow aim to foster reflection about an experiential activity—a simulation, game, role-play, or service-learning or community-engagement experience—or a write-up of such an activity:

- Initially, what goals did you set?
- What strategy did you initially follow for achieving your goals?
- As you immersed yourself in the experience and observed the actions of others, how did you modify your goals and strategies?
- What important actions did you decide to take as you worked toward your goals? Which proved successful? Which, if any, did not work out as you had hoped?
- Did the actions of other characters/players/people surprise you? How did you respond to those actions?
- Did your feelings about yourself or other characters/players/people change during the experience? If so, how?
- How well do you think you performed overall? Evaluate your success in achieving your goals (initial and modified) and the effectiveness of your strategies.
- If you were going through this experience again, what would you do differently?
- How did this experience illustrate the content and learning outcomes of this course?

Conclusion

If your learning outcomes preclude assessing your students' critical thinking skills with objective items, or if you choose not to use objective items, you can assess by designing a constructed-response assignment or exam built around a realistic problem, paradox, puzzle, or disquieting situation. The prompt may take the form of text alone or also include another medium such as a graphic, an audio file, a video, or an animation. Finding discipline-relevant stimuli, vexing problems, head-scratching paradoxes or puzzles, or troublesome situations in the workplace, the community, or the greater world shouldn't be too difficult.

To begin formulating your own critical thinking constructed-response prompts, start by imagining perplexing problems or situations that your students might face during their education or after they graduate. Relevance should shape your selections. Which ones might your students be able to solve—or at least begin to solve—using the critical thinking skills on which your course focuses? Now, draft a constructed-response question or task or a series of related of questions or tasks that would require critical thinking to respond successfully. You may want to modify it in some ways as you think more about the problem or situation.

Once you have written an appropriate constructed-response prompt, you need to decide how you will assess your students' constructed responses. You can choose to design and use a rubric or to develop specifications and "specs grade" your students' products (Nilson, 2015). Chapters 10 and 11, respectively, provide guidance on how best to implement each approach.

ASSESSING CONSTRUCTED
RESPONSES USING
RUBRICS

A fter you develop constructed-response prompts, your next step is determining how you will assess and ultimately grade your students' responses. For this purpose, you have two options. If you decide to grade traditionally on a point system, you develop a rubric. Alternatively, if you prefer to specifications grade (specs grade, for short) your students' work, you develop specifications. This chapter shows you how to do the former, while the next chapter guides you in doing the latter.

Steps for Developing a Rubric

To develop a rubric, you first decide the criteria on which you will assess your students' responses. Limit these to between four and seven criteria. They should include among them one or more of your critical thinking learning outcomes, specifically those that you designed the constructed-response prompt to assess. What skills did you deem most important for your students to demonstrate in *this* constructed-response question or task?

You may have other criteria in mind as well—perhaps following the directions for the assignment; using technical terminology correctly; following an expected organization or format; writing in the style of the discipline; expressing ideas clearly; or integrating appropriate course material, such as certain concepts or principles, into the response. Aside from specific critical thinking skills, what else do you want your students to demonstrate in their responses?

After listing all your assessment criteria, you define your levels of performance and their corresponding point values, assuming you are grading the work. Each level of performance may merit a particular point value or a range of points; a range allows you more flexibility and discretion in grading. (Using letter grades is also an option but one rarely used these days.) If you intend only to provide feedback, then use descriptors instead—for example, high, average, or low mastery; excellent, good, adequate, or needing work; exemplary, competent, developing, or unacceptable; mastery, proficiency, limited proficiency, or no proficiency. Of course, when grading, you can use descriptors along with points.

Next, you decide how to lay out your descriptions of each performance level on each assessment criterion. Will you use a tabular format or an alternative format, where you simply the list key features of each performance level, criterion by criterion? You'll find examples of both in the following section. Will you write your descriptions in phrases or full sentences? After making these decisions, you start drafting your descriptions of the performance for each level on each assessment criterion.

Examples of Critical Thinking Rubrics

Before writing your descriptions, especially for critical thinking, you might examine some proven models, such as these, and consider adapting parts of them to your purposes:

- AAC&U's (2009) critical thinking VALUE rubric
- Facione et al.'s (2011) holistic critical thinking scoring rubric
- Insight Assessment's (2019) evaluating written argumentation rubric
- Northeastern Illinois University's (2006) general education critical thinking rubric
- Washington State University's (2009) critical and integrative thinking rubric

Table 10.1 is a rubric that I composed after studying well over a dozen critical thinking rubrics from many different sources.

Not all the dimensions in this rubric may pertain to your critical thinking question or task. Recall the prompts in chapter 9 asking students to analyze data in Table 8.1, Median Value of Debt for Households, by Type of Debt and Selected Characteristics: 2016 (repeated in the following):

> Refer to the data in the table, Median Value of Debt for Households, by Type of Debt and Selected Characteristics: 2016, to develop your answer to this essay question. Which three of four groups of U.S. households have the worst debt problem, and how did you determine these groups?

TABLE 10.1

A Synthetic Critical Thinking Rubric in Tabular Format

	Mastery	Proficiency	Limited proficiency	No proficiency
Identifies the key problem, issue, or argument	Accurately identifies all aspects of the key problem, issue, or argument	Accurately identifies almost all aspects of the key problem, issue, or argument	Accurately identifies some aspects of the key problem, issue, or argument	Misrepresents or fails to identify the key problem, issue, or argument
Identifies, analyzes, and assesses different and opposing claims	Accurately identifies, analyzes, and assesses all the salient alternative claims	Accurately identifies, analyzes, and assesses some of the salient alternative claims	Describes some of the salient alternative claims but fails to analyze or assess them	Misses or misrepresents most of the salient claims; makes illogical or fallacious statements
Interprets data, evidence, graphics, results, and so on	Accurately interprets all the data, evidence, graphics, results, and so on	Accurately interprets nearly all the data, evidence, graphics, results, and so on	Accurately interprets some of the data, evidence, graphics, results, and so on	Misinterprets all or almost all the data, evidence, graphics, results, and so on
Explains and gives reasons for the approach, procedures, and results	Thoroughly explains and gives reasons for the approach, procedures, and results	Explains and gives reasons for the approach, procedures, and results, but misses some key points	Partially explains and gives reasons for the approach, procedures, and results	Fails to explain and give reasons for the approach, procedures, and results
Uses logical reasoning and evidence to come to a conclusion	Uses logical reasoning and all the available evidence to come to a conclusion	Uses logical reasoning and some of the available evidence to come to a conclusion	Makes some logical errors and misses key evidence in coming to a conclusion	Ignores logic or evidence in coming to a conclusion; may exhibit self-interest or close-mindedness

Reminder: The true burden of a household's debt is relative to that household's income and wealth. In addition, be aware that secured debt is less burdensome that unsecured debt. Let's take a household holding secured debts of $200,000 and unsecured debts of $20,000 with an annual income in the highest quintile and a net worth of $1 million. This is a total debt value of $220,000. Let's take another household holding secured debts of $30,000 and unsecured debt of $10,000 with an annual income in the lowest quintile and a net worth of $15,000. This is a total debt value of $40,000. Which household is more burdened by debt? The second household is because, compared to the former household, its debts are relatively larger than its annual income and net worth. In addition, the second household has relatively more unsecured debt, even though it is half of what the former holds. Keep these economic complexities in mind as you consider the debt problems of various groups and justify your determination of the most debt-burdened.

To assess your students' responses to this critical thinking prompt, you would probably want to focus on four of the five criteria in Table 10.1: identifies the key problem, issue, or argument; interprets data, evidence, statements, results, and so on; explains and gives reasons for the approach, procedures, and results; and uses logical reasoning and evidence to come to a conclusion. The fifth criterion—identifies, analyzes, and assesses different and opposing claims—seems not to apply here because the prompt does not pose competing points of view. Don't forget that you may choose to add to your rubric other criteria that do not address critical thinking skills.

Let's see how the synthetic rubric in Table 10.1 applies to some of the upgraded prompts (Nilson, 2016a Unit 4.1; reprinted with permission from Magna Publications) in the preceding section:

Some people argue that the United States is following the same path of decline as the Roman Empire. Write a critical examination of this claim analyzing how the United States is and is not declining due to similar factors.

This prompt does indeed suggest the reality of competing points of view: that the United States is declining due to similar factors that led to the Roman Empire to decline, and that the United States is *not* declining, at least not due to similar factors. You may notice that the contrary claim is somewhat implicit. This dispute justifies using all five criteria to assess students' responses to this critical thinking challenge: identifies the key problem, issue, or argument; identifies, analyzes, and assesses different and opposing claims; interprets data, evidence, statements, results, and so on; explains and gives reasons for the approach, procedures, and results; and uses logical reasoning and evidence to come to a conclusion.

> After the first injection of an immunotherapy program, you notice a large, red wheal on your patient's arm. Then the patient begins coughing and expiratory wheezing. What series of interventions should you implement? Justify your interventions and their sequence.

Not all the criteria in the synthetic rubric applies to this prompt. While the symptoms presented may be ambiguous, there are no clear competing points of view and, therefore, no place for identifying, analyzing, and assessing different and opposing claims. In addition, the prompt lays out the key problem or issue, so students need not identify it. Still, three criteria remain important: interprets data, evidence, statements, results, and so on; explains and gives reasons for the approach, procedures, and results; and uses logical reasoning and evidence to come to a conclusion.

> The education of the working and middle classes has been increasing for several decades while their income has been flat or decreasing for the past two decades. How can you resolve this trend with the well-established positive relationship between education and income? (Consider other factors that may affect income.)

This prompt raises an interesting paradox and asks students to resolve it. Here, a paradox denotes an inconsistency between the findings of different studies, but not a disagreement that implies different or opposing claims. A student's response should identify this as the key problem or issue, which is one criterion in the synthesized rubric. From this point, three of the remaining four criteria apply: interprets data, evidence, statements, results, and so on; explains and gives reasons for the approach, procedures, and results; and uses logical reasoning and evidence to come to a conclusion.

> Some geoscientists maintain that the mega-magna chamber below Yellowstone National Park is leaking increasing amounts of sulfur dioxide into the atmosphere and will cause a mass extinction within 70,000 years. They rest this claim on the mass extinction that happened 250 million years ago. Why or why not do you accept this claim? To what extent are the hydrospheric, atmospheric, and biospheric conditions comparable to those 250 million years ago?

While the prompt makes only one claim explicit, the opposing claim—that Yellowstone's activity will *not* cause a mass extinction within 70,000 years—is implicit. Given these competing points of view, all five criteria apply: identifies the key problem, issue, or argument; identifies, analyzes, and assesses different and opposing claims; interprets data, evidence, statements, results, and so on; explains and gives reasons for the approach, procedures, and results; and uses logical reasoning and evidence to come to a conclusion.

The context-rich physics problem about Martian rocks being found on Earth doesn't fit quite as well with the synthetic rubric. It does not present, explicitly or implicitly, different or opposing claims, although students may debate different approaches to the problem in their mind or among their peers before they start solving. However, a solid solution does involve these four criteria: identifying the key problem, issue, or argument; interpreting data, evidence, statements, results, and so on; explaining and giving reasons for one's approach, procedures, and results; and using logical reasoning and evidence to come to a conclusion. Arriving at an accurate solution also entails correct calculations—specifically of the magnitude of the rock's velocity as a function of its distance from the volcano and the height of the volcano for the rock farthest from the volcano—and standard critical thinking rubrics exclude such cognitive tasks. This criterion would have to be added.

Finally, you can decide whether you will use the alternative type of rubric that is headed by "does all/almost all/most of these." As you descend the levels, the descriptors shade from highly positive to highly negative. For a model, see Figure 10.1, which displays the same synthetic rubric shown in Table 10.1 but in alternative format. To design your own, start by listing the criteria for each level and value.

Keep in mind that once you distribute your rubric to your students as your grading guide, you cannot ethically change it. However, like many instructors, you may want to make adjustments to it after using it to grade.

While rubrics incorporate comments to students, you may want to add more personalized feedback. The literature gives somewhat conflicting guidance. Some scholars advise balancing positive and negative comments and explaining why a line of reasoning merits praise or correction (Taylor, 2010). Others recommend focusing comments on ways that students can improve their work in relation to your rubric criteria and praising, not the product itself, but the effort students put forth and the process they followed in completing the product (Coffield, 2014; Dweck, 2007; Halvorson, 2014). Either way, if you're concerned that your students may not read your feedback, ask

Figure 10.1. The synthetic critical thinking rubric in alternative format.

Mastery—Does all or almost all of the following:

- Accurately identifies the key problem, issue, or argument
- Accurately identifies, analyzes, and assesses all the salient alternative claims
- Accurately interprets all the data, evidence, graphics, results, and so on
- Thoroughly explains and gives reasons for the approach, procedures, and results
- Uses logical reasoning and all the available evidence to come to a conclusion

Proficiency—Does most of the following:

- Accurately identifies almost all aspects of the key problem, issue, or argument
- Accurately identifies, analyzes, and assesses some of the salient alternative claims
- Accurately interprets nearly all the data, evidence, graphics, results, and so on
- Explains and gives reasons for the approach, procedures, and results, but misses one or two key points
- Uses logical reasoning and some of the available evidence to come to a conclusion

Limited proficiency—Does most of the following:

- Accurately identifies some aspects of the key problem, issue, or argument
- Describes some of the salient alternative claims but fails to analyze or assess them
- Accurately interprets some of the data, evidence, graphics, results, and so on
- Partially explains and gives reasons for the approach, procedures, and results
- Makes some logical errors and misses key evidence in coming to a conclusion

No proficiency—Does all or almost all the following:

- Misrepresents or fails to identify the key problem, issue, or argument
- Misses or misrepresents most of the salient claims. Makes illogical or fallacious statements
- Misinterprets all or almost all the data, evidence, graphics, results, and so on
- Fails to explain and give reasons for the approach, procedures, and results
- Ignores logic or evidence in coming to a conclusion; may exhibit self-interest or close-mindedness

them to paraphrase your comments back to you as a follow-up assignment. You may find that in some cases you didn't communicate what you intended.

Conclusion

If you decide to assess your students' critical thinking skills with a constructed-response assignment or exam and you want to grade traditionally using a point system, your best option is to design a rubric. Start by deciding on four to seven criteria for assessing your students' responses, where at least some of the criteria reflect the critical thinking learning outcomes that you want your students to demonstrate in this particular constructed response. You then describe each level of performance on each criterion and assign to each level a point value—a specific number of points or a range of points.

If you have grown tired of students challenging your assignment of points to their work, you have an alternative assessment system: specifications grading, or "specs grading" for short. The next chapter addresses this system, including how to develop specifications for assessing your students' products.

11

ASSESSING CONSTRUCTED
RESPONSES USING
SPECIFICATIONS
GRADING

I f you are among the many faculty members who find our traditional grading system cumbersome and unhelpful to students, you do have an alternative: specifications ("specs") grading (Nilson, 2015). Because I wrote so
extensively on this topic, I will give only a brief summary of the system here
and focus on its application in assessing critical thinking. When you think
of specs, consider the way a computer program must meet certain minimum
specs: It must run, first of all; it must perform the task that it was designed for;
and it must not exceed a given code length or operation time. A program either
passes or fails to meet these requirements. In the same way, you can set specifications for an assignment or an exam. These specs constitute a one-level rubric.

Two Essential Elements of Specs Grading

Specs grading relies on pass/fail grading and second chances for students.
With respect to the former element, you assess student work (all of it or
whatever work you choose) on a pass/fail, credit/no credit basis. A piece of
work "passes" or receives credit if it meets all the specifications (required
components or qualities) that you have set for the work. If full credit is
10 points, the work merits either 10 points or 0 points—no partial credit.
(Unfortunately, some students hand in substandard work knowing that
partial credit will save them from a failing grade on the assignment or in
the course.) The specifications that you require should offer evidence of a
student's achievement of one or more of your course learning outcomes.

Specs grading for assignments and exams resembles competency-based education at the program level, where program faculty lay out the specs for evidence of having achieved a competency, or outcome. A student performs at that level and passes or does not and fails, at least on that attempt.

In the traditional grading system, passing a course with enough points overall provides no guarantee that a student has achieved any of the promised outcomes. Does a C mean that the student has achieved some of the outcomes and not others? If so, which ones haven't been achieved, and why is this student passing the course? For that matter, what does a B mean in terms of what a student is and is not able to do? Does an A signify that a student has achieved all the outcomes at a high level, or most of them, or what? It's little wonder that accreditors and employers pay scant attention to our traditionally calculated grades.

The specs-grading system also allows a limited number of second chances; I call them "tokens," but you can call them whatever you would prefer. Each student starts your course with, let's say, three of them and can use one to revise a failed assignment, retake a failed or missed test, turn in an assignment 24 hours late without penalty, take an excused absence from class, or whatever other purpose makes sense in your course. If you'd like, you can reward students with the most unused tokens at the end of the term—perhaps with an inexpensive gift certificate at a local restaurant. Incidentally, these are virtual, not physical, tokens, and you keep track of them in your grade book. Otherwise, a black market may spring up among some of your students!

To pass or get credit, students must know *exactly* what they have to do in an assignment or exam to pass—that is, they must read and understand the specs. Otherwise, their work will probably fail, entailing some degree of cost even with low-stakes quizzes or homework. Therefore, before students begin a work, we must communicate our expectations very clearly and carefully—more clearly and carefully than the brief descriptions that we give in multilevel rubrics. In addition, we have to prioritize a limited number of requirements for students to focus on. This clarity removes the guesswork and mind-reading from our assessment instruments, lowering students' stress and increasing their motivation (evidence in Nilson, 2015).

Specs grading promises to restore rigor by raising the bar for acceptable student performance because C-level work no longer passes. Your aim is to require at least a B-level performance as passing. If you already have a rubric that works well for it, you can take the highest-scoring row and the one below it as guides. For quizzes and exams, you simply require a minimum score of 80%. If you have essays on exams, you can set specs for them if you wish.

Writing Specs for Constructed Responses

For fairly short assignments, writing specs is as easy as asking a clear question or two and giving a minimum word or sentence requirement for the response. You might also show your students a couple of examples of acceptable and unacceptable work to ensure that they understand the specs (e.g., answering all the questions and meeting or exceeding the minimum length). In her Management Information Systems (MIS) course, Professor Kathleen Kegley (personal communication, January 5, 2009) assigned various short writing exercises to ensure that her students completed and demonstrated some understanding of the readings—for example:

- Write about 10 sentences in your own words summarizing the most important points in the _____ article.
- Find and briefly summarize an article in the *Wall Street Journal* related to MIS.
- After reading the _____ article, pick out five new concepts that you learned and define them in your own words.
- Select two items of interest to you at _____ website and briefly describe the impact they can have on business.
- Read one other article at this website and summarize what you learned in five to eight sentences.

Determining the specs for longer assignments such as papers, projects, and oral presentations involve more thought. Nilson (2015) furnishes examples, but the ones here concentrate on specs that demonstrate critical thinking skills in addition to disciplinary knowledge. You might tailor the specs to each assignment or essay test question rather than trying to use a standard critical thinking rubric. Keep in mind that your specs will lay out all the features of a work to which you would give at least a B, and these features may include the organization or format that you would like to see (e.g., the focus of the introduction or conclusion). Let's start with the upgraded prompts for the assignments and essays (Nilson, 2016a, Unit 4.1; reprinted with permission from Magna Publications) and the context-rich problem in the previous chapter. Note that all the sets of specs include the minimum word length except the one for the context-rich problem (the one about Martian rocks).

Prompt:

> Some people argue that the United States is following the same path of decline as the Roman Empire. Write a critical examination of this claim

analyzing how the United States is and is not declining due to similar factors.

Possible specs:

- Introductory paragraph states what your essay is going to do, paragraph by paragraph.
- Essay makes at least six valid comparisons between the Roman Empire as it was declining and the recent and contemporary United States—at least two that show similarities and at least two that show differences.
- All the information provided about Roman Empire as it was declining and about the recent and contemporary United States is accurate.
- Concluding paragraph evaluates the validity of the claim that the United States is following the same path of decline as the Roman Empire.
- The minimum length is 500 words.

Prompt:

After the first injection of an immunotherapy program, you notice a large, red wheal on your patient's arm. Then the patient begins coughing and expiratory wheezing. What series of interventions should you implement? Justify your interventions and their sequence.

Possible specs:

- Essay describes an ordered series of at least four interventions, all of which are appropriate and properly sequenced.
- Essay justifies the sequenced series in reference to urgency, the three most likely sources of the problem, and the recommended immediate treatments for the three most likely problems.
- The minimum length is 500 words.

Prompt:

The education of the working and middle classes has been increasing for several decades while their income has been flat or decreasing for the past two decades. How can you resolve this trend with the well established positive relationship between education and income? (Consider other factors that may affect income.)

Possible specs:

- Paper states the key reason why the paradox (apparent contradiction) exists.
- Paper analyzes how at least five societal factors or trends affect the income of the working and middle classes.
- Paper explains the recent relevant changes in these factors.
- Paper ties these recent relevant changes to the lagging income of the working and middle classes.
- The minimum length is 1,000 words.

Prompt:

Some geoscientists maintain that the mega-magna chamber below Yellowstone National Park is leaking increasing amounts of sulfur dioxide into the atmosphere and will cause a mass extinction within 70,000 years. They rest this claim on the mass extinction that happened 250 million years ago. Why or why not do you accept this claim? To what extent are the hydrospheric, atmospheric, and biospheric conditions comparable to those 250 million years ago?

Possible specs:

- Report accurately describes the known causes of the mass extinction that happened 250 million years.
- Report accurately describes the known characteristics of this mass extinction.
- Report accurately analyzes the known hydrospheric, atmospheric, and biospheric conditions surrounding this mass extinction.
- Report accurately compares the known conditions surrounding the mass extinction to (a) the hydrospheric, atmospheric, and biospheric conditions today and (b) those projected for the next 70,000 years.
- Report includes the known amount and rate of sulfur dioxide being released into the atmosphere from the mega-magna chamber below Yellowstone National Park since its last major eruption about 640,000 years ago.
- Report concludes with an evaluation of the claim that the mega-magna chamber below Yellowstone will leak enough sulfur dioxide into the atmosphere to cause a mass extinction within 70,000 years.
- The minimum length is 750 words.

Recall the complex physics problem about Martian rocks being found on Earth (p. 100, this volume). This critical thinking assessment can also have specs, although a minimum word length makes less sense in this context.

Possible specs:

- Solution begins by listing the knowns, unknowns, and assumptions, and the information given is correct.
- Solution includes at least one drawing.
- Solution correctly calculates the magnitude of the rock's velocity as a function of its distance from the volcano and the height of the volcano for the rock farthest from the volcano.
- Solution describes sound reasoning behind every step of the calculation.
- Solution concludes with an evaluation of the friend's claim that large Martian volcanoes shot off the Martian rocks that were found on Earth.

With specs grading, the bulk of your assessment work, which is formulating the specs, is upfront, and you can do it before the term begins. Grading involves examining your students' products only for the presence of those specs. If the specs are all met in a product, it passes. If any are missing, you simply note which one(s), and the work fails. As your time permits, you can give more personalized feedback. In fact, your students may pay more attention to it because you're not giving it to justify your taking off points, as instructors often do in traditional grading (evidence in Nilson, 2015). Of course, for surrendering a token (if available), a student may revise a work that fails.

Determining Letter Grades at the End of a Course

How does specs grading allow you to end a course with letter grades for your students? You can maintain a point-based system where each passed assignment and test accrues so many points toward a total number on which the final grade is based. But this is not your only option, nor might it be your best one. Unfortunately, point totals do not map onto outcomes. They do not say what a student is and is not able to do at the end of a course. A point total of 70, 82, or 91 out of 100 indicates very little about a student's competencies.

The alternative—and the vast majority of faculty who use specs grading have adopted it—is to put together "bundles" of assessments, where each bundle earns a different final course grade. Any given bundle contains several student products, each of which is graded pass/fail against a set of specs. As part of your course design, you determine the assignments and tests to put in each bundle. For higher grades, the bundles should require more work (e.g., more assignments and tests), or more challenging work, or both. More challenging work means more advanced, more difficult, or higher-level in terms of the cognitive demands. Often the bundle associated with a final grade of D serves as a base, with the C bundle adding one or more assessments to the D bundle, the B bundle adding one or more assessments to the C bundle, and the A bundle adding one or more assessments to the B bundle.

Bundling assessments holds multiple advantages for both students and instructors. First, students can study the bundles at the beginning of the course and select the final grade they are going to work toward. They can consider the workload and difficulty level of each bundle, their interest in the subject matter, the time they expect to have available for the course, and the grade they actually need. Having such choice serves as a great motivator. You need not worry that all students will vie for an A. They may consider the required amount of time and the difficulty not worth it to them, and we should respect this decision. However, we should encourage our under-represented, underprepared, and first-generation students to aim for an A because they may lack confidence and underestimate their capabilities.

Second, you can design a bundle to indicate that a student has achieved one or more course learning outcomes. Bundles for higher grades may assess more outcomes (e.g., more skills and/or knowledge), or more advanced/difficult ones to achieve (e.g., higher-level cognitive outcomes), or both. To illustrate using Bloom's taxonomy of cognitive operations, completing a bundle for a C may require students to demonstrate only knowledge and comprehension of the material; completing a B bundle may demand that they also can apply and analyze that material; completing an A bundle may additionally require that they can synthesize and evaluate the material. If students have to achieve any early-in-the-term outcomes before they can achieve later outcomes, the bundles should be sequenced. In fact, you should schedule the due dates for bundles and their component assessments throughout the term to prevent your having to grade a deluge of work at the end of the term.

Third, bundling allows you to easily add learning value to your core assessments—perhaps a cocurricular activity such as attending a concert, play, museum, or conference; a reflective meta-assignment (see the next subsection) to enhance your students' self-regulated learning skills; a postexam reflection to help your students avoid the same mistakes on the next exam;

or a creative or self-directed task related to your core assessment that takes advantage of your students' personal or career interests, artistic talents, or desire to innovate.

A final advantage: Bundles make the grading process easier, quicker, and less stressful. You can put them together to increase your students' time on task or elevate their level of thinking without making the grading structure more complex. You need not calculate points, and you don't need to deal with students who try to argue for additional points. Rather, you simply assess a set of assignments and tests to see if any piece is missing or falls short of your requirements. If this happens, you can return the work to the student to be revised if they have a token available for this purpose.

If specs grading interests you, you can find out much more about it and see many examples of specs and specs-graded courses in Nilson (2015). As with other major course changes, you can start small and ease into it— perhaps by specs grading only some of your students' work. Or you can adopt only parts of the system and keep some features of traditional grading.

Conclusion

Specs grading offers a viable alternative strategy for assessing and grading your students' performance in your courses. It streamlines your task of assessing their constructed responses requiring critical thinking (or any other skill), reduces both your own and your students' stress, and confers other advantages as well, including making students' course grades meaningful indicators of the learning outcomes they have achieved. Developing good specs for an assignment or essay test is quite easy, whether or not you have a multilevel rubric to work from. You simply have to ask yourself exactly what you want your students to demonstrate that they can do.

12

CRITICAL THINKING
AND THE PROMISE OF
HIGHER EDUCATION

Not long ago, the main motivation for attending college focused less on obtaining gainful employment or more material goods and more on becoming a wiser and more open-minded, inquisitive, and self-actualizing person. During this time, the economy was stronger, wages and salaries relatively higher, upward mobility more likely, economic inequality less extreme, and higher education less important to material well-being. Certainly, poverty existed, but very little among the gainfully employed. There were few or no "working poor." Now, employment offers much less assurance of economic security and material survival; many working young people cannot afford to move out of their parents' home and strike out on their own. And nothing turns our attention away from personal growth, development, and self-realization like threats to our physiological welfare and safety (Maslow, 1954).

Surveys of first-year undergraduate students document the outcome of this economic shift. In the mid to late 1960s, students attended college more to optimize the quality of their lives than to maximize their eventual paychecks. Specifically, 86% of freshmen in 1967 responded that their main motivation for attending was to develop a meaningful philosophy of life (Hong, 2004). This goal echoes what a liberal arts education offers, and critical thinking skills rank among those benefits. Today, about the same percentage select financial reasons for attending college: 84.9% "to get a better job" and 71.8% "to make more money" (Stolzenberg et al., 2018, p. 36). Missing from the table is developing a meaningful philosophy of life because so few respondents cite it.

The first chapter of this book gave a list of hopefully compelling reasons for today's students to learn critical thinking. We must never forget nor let our students miss the fact that the real payoffs of learning and practicing critical thinking lie far beyond the classroom. It is an everyday life skill, like clear communication and quantitative reasoning, that reaps rewards in many life contexts. It should inform a person's consumer, political, financial, occupational, ethical, medical, and legal decisions (Brookfield, 2012b; Browne & Keeley, 2018; Facione, 2011, 2020; Nisbett, 1993; Nosich, 2012).

Critical thinking can even help one make better personal choices, such as who to trust, who to commit to, and how to discipline children. Yes, all life decisions have a strong emotional component, but it helps to be able to distinguish a rational case from an emotional plea for taking action. News commentators, politicians, advertisers, and various authorities throw fallacious arguments at us all day, and most people fall for them, even though the messages may contradict each other. Our students need to know that critical thinking is a real-world skill that is well worth transferring. It is their only protection against being duped and manipulated on a daily basis.

Where We Have Traveled

Opening with the tremendous, lifelong payoffs of critical thinking, this book moved to the relevant literature—a fragmented, adisciplinary collection of definitions, types of assumptions, standards, elements of thought, skills, biases, intellectual traits, stages, and questions to help students develop their critical thinking skills. Not to discredit the profound insights within these frameworks, but the literature as a whole can confuse instructors who want to apply it. The frameworks do not build on each other, and each proceeds as if the others do not exist.

Chapter 3 enumerated 10 reasons why critical thinking is so challenging to teach, starting the nature of the literature. Still, the frameworks overlap on many counts, and the chapter identified their common ground and presented a synthesis of some general principles. The first of these was a "pocket" definition of *critical thinking* as interpretation, analysis, and evaluation leading to a decision or problem solution. Other principles zeroed in on additional challenges of teaching critical thinking: the need for its intentional, explicit integration into a course; the requirement of disputed claims in the course's content; the psychological barriers to critical thinking; the widespread misconceptions about it; its dependency on self-regulation, good character, and emotional health; its esoteric vocabulary; and its reliance on thought-demanding questions, which most students resist answering.

Fortunately, these challenges can be overcome. Chapter 3 offered a few strategies and solutions, but most of them appeared in later in the book. Chapter 4 handled the task of infusing critical thinking into a course by suggesting discipline-relevant student learning outcomes, some that already characterize many courses but are not identified as critical thinking outcomes. The next three chapters concentrated on meeting teaching challenges. Chapter 5 addressed how to familiarize students with the vocabulary, acquaint them with the process of critical thinking, foster their reflection and self-regulation, and develop their character. Chapter 6 focused on questions to pose to students, beginning with the questions and tasks recommended by each of the major frameworks summarized in chapter 2 and arriving at a synthesized "master list" of critical thinking questions. This chapter also explained Socratic questioning for instructors who feel less need to plan out classes. Finishing up the teaching portion of the book, chapter 7 detailed the most effective methods for helping students learn how to think critically, along with the most relevant questions to incorporate into these learning activities and experiences. It also suggested ways and models to advance students' skills through a course.

Chapters 8 through 11 dealt with assessment and grading. Many faculty may be surprised to learn that objective items can test so many critical thinking skills, as chapter 8 demonstrated. The more predictable option is having students "construct" responses to questions and task prompts, and chapter 9 homed in on the most effective kinds of questions and prompts for assessing critical thinking. With either type of assessment, you are not likely to find appropriate objective items and constructed response prompts in test banks or instructor manuals. So the respective chapters supplied guidelines for developing your own. Finally, chapters 10 and 11 explained two distinct ways to assess students' constructed responses— with a rubric or with specifications—and advised how to write each type of criteria.

Hopefully, you feel that you have left the critical thinking thicket behind you and have arrived at a series of clearings while reading this book. Teaching critical thinking cannot be boiled down to a paint-by-numbers procedure, but now you should know the decisions that you need to make—about learning outcomes, the vocabulary to teach, teaching methods, questions to pose, self-regulated learning activities, assessments, and grading—and the options that you have to choose from. You have all the tools you need to feel confident that you can intelligently infuse critical thinking into one or more of your courses.

The Possible Costs of Critical Thinking and Speaking the Truth

We have examined the definitions of critical thinking of scholars who have made themselves famous for their critical thinking frameworks. However, other scholars have also offered definitions more closely related to truth-finding. According to Dr. Will Joel Friedman (2019), a clinical psychologist, "Critical thinking is not critical, just looking for truth and reality. [It is] the heart of asking questions that reveal 'what is'" (para. 1). Nihon University's philosophy professor Lajos L. Brons (n.d.) concurs: "[C]ritical thinking is aiming for truth" (p. 24). So does writer, analyst, and designer Michael Alwill (2018), who contends, "There is truth and there is belief, and the greatest tool humans have to differentiate between the two—and to differentiate between truth and falsehood—is critical thinking" (para. 65).

Thinkers from all walks of life endorse critical thinking as the pathway to the truth, at least the truth in this physical, sensory dimension. (Augustine notwithstanding, critical thinking may not take you that far in the religious or spiritual realms.) Jesus reputedly said to his disciples, "The truth shall set you free" (John 8:32). Presumably, he meant free from fears while preaching his message. Indeed, his disciples had good reasons to fear the reactions of local high priests, Roman government leaders, and Middle Eastern communities.

Not to deny the bounty of benefits that comes with critical thinking, but history tells us again and again that not all people want to hear the truth or want others to hear it. You can be imprisoned, exiled, or even killed for exercising critical thinking and speaking the truth.

Consider the Italian astronomer and physicist Galileo Galilei (1564–1642), a familiar example. He published research in support of the Copernican theory that the Earth revolves around the Sun. Endorsing scripture that placed the Earth at the center of the universe, the Catholic Church condemned Galileo's "belief" as heretical and banned his writings. He spent the last 9 years of his life under house arrest.

A less familiar example is that of Persian medical researcher and "Renaissance man" Muhammad ibn Zakariyā Rāzī (Rhazes) (865–925) who brought Western teachings, including the works of Hippocrates and Galen, to the Arabic world. His writings caught the critical eye of a Muslim priest who had him beaten over the head with his manuscript, causing him to go blind and ending his medical practice.

Another lesser-known physician, this one from Spain, Michael Servetus (1511[?]–1553) discovered and wrote about pulmonary circulation. But he also published his recommendations on reforming Christianity. While he narrowly escaped the Spanish Inquisition by moving to Switzerland, he encountered the Protestant Inquisition there, where John Calvin had him arrested, tortured, and burned at the stake.

A publisher of scientific papers who founded the Royal Society in London, Henry Oldenburg (1619–1677) corresponded with scientists all over Europe in search of outstanding papers to publish. All those letters aroused the suspicion of English authorities, who thought he was a spy and imprisoned him in the Tower of London.

In 1912 Alfred Wegener (1880–1930), a German meteorologist and geophysicist, set forth the theory of continental drift. He backed it up with a wealth of evidence, including the existence of duplicate plants and animal fossils, similar rock formations, and look-alike mountain ranges on different continents, as well as the puzzle-like fit between continents across the Atlantic Ocean. Despite garnering some support in pockets of the scientific community, the leading geologists of the time viciously mocked him and his theory, preferring instead an unsubstantiated theory of sunken land bridges between the continents.

Such suppression for bearing witness to the truth has continued into the 21st century. Look at Edward Snowden (2019), now living in exile since 2013 because he exposed U.S. intelligence services for conducting the mass surveillance and storage of worldwide digital communications. Look at the Saudi Arabian author and columnist for *The Washington Post*, Jamal Khashoggi, who was assassinated on October 2, 2018, at the Saudi consulate in Istanbul, Turkey. His alleged killers had close ties to the top levels of the Saudi government and Crown Prince Mohammed bin Salman, who resented Khashoggi for publishing critiques of his policies. In fact, you can find entire web sites about the journalists killed in Afghanistan, Brazil, Ecuador, Kashmir, Libya, Mexico, Slovakia, Syria, and the United States in 2018 alone—some by their own government and others by extremist groups, organized crime, or motivated individuals (Mohdin & van der Zee, 2018; Vick, 2019).

What does all this suppression have to do with higher education? Well-educated people seem to be the ones most likely to speak out or act against corrupt, closed-minded, or threatened power-elites. Where would we be without knowledgeable and intellectually courageous individuals? Take your pick of these dystopian novels for predictive insight: *The Handmaid's Tale* (Atwood, 1985), *Fahrenheit 451* (Bradbury, 1953), *Red Rising* (Brown, 2014), *The Hunger Games* (Collins, 2008), *Brave New World* (Huxley, 1932), *The Giver* (Lowry, 1993), *Animal Farm* (Orwell, 1945), *Nineteen Eighty-Four* (Orwell, 1949), or *Snow Crash* (Stephenson, 1992). No doubt, some if not all of the authors intended their books as warnings of creeping authoritarianism, intensifying indoctrination, increasing censorship, and diminishing freedoms. Some of these novels have been popularized in movies.

Because these novels are fictional—at the moment anyway—your students may miss their immediate relevance. Perhaps these quotations from Tsipursky and Ward (2020) bring the implications of political dishonesty closer to home:

> If politicians can win by telling lies, then they do not need to care about serving the true interests of the citizens. Without a norm of truthfulness as a basic check on the behavior of politicians, they can steal taxpayer money and collude with corporate interests to line their own pockets. Worse, they can use lies to keep power in an authoritarian manner by: stuffing ballots and stealing elections, arresting those who oppose them on trumped up charges, and murdering journalists or other opponents who try and expose their lies. These abuses of power are not dystopian fantasies. They are taking place today in many powerful nations the world over, including some that used to be democracies. (p. 9)

> Our age-old thinking and feeling patterns that evolved on the African savannah have left us vulnerable in the 21st century to misinformation and fake news spread via social and online media. . . .We face the same struggle today, not for dominance on the grasslands, but for control of the territory of our own minds. For this purpose, this book has taken the insights of behavioral science research and forged them into a set of tools you can use for spotting lies and thinking errors and learning to resist them. (Tsipursky & Ward, 2020, p. 239)

If you are concerned about telling your students the costs that they may face for speaking the truth, enlighten them about the societal consequences of their *not* standing up for the truth.

Our freedom lies in our awareness of the patterns of human cognition, their exploitability, and the worldwide pandemic of dishonesty in the pursuit of power and money. This awareness springs from not only knowledge but also critical thinking. And it has generated several successful movements—for environmental protection, conservation, sustainability, recycling, and stronger vehicle safety standards, to name a few—in our time. Therefore, we can take heart in knowing that we are not doomed to blindness and manipulation.

The Pledge

Intentional Insights is an educational nonprofit, unaffiliated with any political group, that has as its the goal "promoting science-based truth-seeking, rational thinking, and wise decision-making" (Intentional Insights, 2017, para. 1). Gleb Tsipursky, a former member of the history faculty at Ohio State

University, founded the organization, of which he is president. He also code-veloped the Pro-Truth Pledge (n.d.) as an effort to combat misinformation and advance truth. Its website documents the many media that have featured the pledge and some of its impact. It also invites people to take the pledge themselves (reprinted with permission from G. Tsipursky from https://www .protruthpledge.org/):

I Pledge My Earnest Efforts to:

Share truth

- Verify: Fact-check information to confirm it is true before accepting and sharing it.
- Balance: Share the whole truth, even if some aspects do not support my opinion.
- Cite: Share my sources so that others can verify my information.
- Clarify: Distinguish between my opinion and the facts.

Honor truth

- Acknowledge: Acknowledge when others share true information, even when we disagree otherwise.
- Reevaluate: Reevaluate if my information is challenged, retract it if I cannot verify it.
- Defend: Defend others when they come under attack for sharing true information, even when we disagree otherwise.
- Align: Align my opinions and my actions with true information.

Encourage truth

- Fix: Ask people to retract information that reliable sources have dis-proved even if they are my allies.
- Educate: Compassionately inform those around me to stop using unreliable sources even if these sources support my opinion.
- Defer: Recognize the opinions of experts as more likely to be accurate when the facts are disputed.
- Celebrate: Celebrate those who retract incorrect statements and update their beliefs toward the truth.

Tsipursky and Ward (2020) promise psychological, social, and moral benefits to those who take the pledge:

All pledge-takers—private citizens and public figures—gain the benefits of cultivating socially beneficial habits of mind, word, and deed. All gain the pride and self-satisfaction of standing up for truth and fighting lies. All gain the benefit of being role models for others. All gain the benefits of building a more truth-driven public culture, and fighting the pollution of truth in politics. (p. 164)

The website (https://www.protruthpledge.org/) contains links to the definition of misinformation, a clarification of expert opinion, help with fact-checking (see also chapter 1, this volume), and the like, making this a truly educational site. While it doesn't refer to critical thinking per se, it implicitly encourages it. Depending on your emphasis on critical thinking in your course, you might recommend the pledge website to your students and ask them to consider taking the pledge. You might also urge them to pressure political leaders to take this pledge, because doing so does make a difference in the behavior of the pledge-takers (Tsipursky & Ward, 2020).

Discussion Activities for Various Purposes

To Motivate Preparation

Discussion Activity	Description
Written homework on assigned reading (or video or podcast)	Students bring in a summary of key points, questions, answers to study or reflective questions, quotations, outline, double-journal of public and private reactions, or passages they see as central, puzzling, novel, interesting, or provocative. Usually worth credit but not graded.
Discussion on discussion	Students discuss the elements of a good discussion and the qualities of a good discussion participant.
Change-your-mind debate	Students prepare and deliver a compelling, evidence-based argument for either the side they select or the opposing side to sway a "neutral" group, which is charged with asking each side challenging questions.
Simulation debate	Students role-play different positions with varying points of view or interests.
Prepared answers to discussion questions	You provide discussion questions before class and ask students to prepare answers as homework. For small-group work, members select the best answers as a group.
Deliberative dialogue	Students write analyses and appraisals of the positions in the readings. In class, they systematically share and listen to different ideas and points of view and then consider and evaluate the various sides. (This is especially useful for discussing sensitive or controversial topics.)

To Encourage Active Listening

Discussion Activity	Description
Note-taking on discussion	Students take notes on discussion, which works best if you scaffold by pointing out important milestones and integrate discussion material into quizzes, exams, and assignments.
Reporting out	One small-group member gives an oral summary of the group discussion (progress, conclusions, or answers), which works best if you randomly call on a few groups and randomly select the spokesperson within each group.
Minute paper	Students write responses to one or more reflective prompts, such as (a) the most important, valuable, or useful thing(s) they learned during the discussion; (b) the most unexpected or surprising thing(s) they learned; or (c) the material they found most confusing.
Fishbowl	A smaller group of students discusses a topic while a larger group quietly listens for understanding and may take notes. The latter group summarizes the former group's ideas and builds on them when the groups switch roles.
Comment summarizing	You ask a student to summarize and build on another student's contribution.
Deliberative dialogue	See first section in this appendix, "To Motivate Preparation."

To Increase or Broaden Participation

Discussion Activity	Description
Reporting out	See "To Encourage Active Listening"
Minute paper	See "To Encourage Active Listening"
Discussion on discussion	See "To Motivate Preparation"
Gallery walk (rotating stations)	You place sheets of paper around the room, each with a different prompt (e.g., question, problem, brainstorming task, graphic to draw) and assign four to five students to each sheet of paper. You give the groups 3 to 5 minutes to respond to the prompt individually or as a group. Then the groups rotate to a new sheet/prompt and repeat the process, generating new responses. After all groups visit each sheet, they walk around the "gallery" to read and comment on all the responses.
Change-your-mind debate	See "To Motivate Preparation"
Simulation debate	See "To Motivate Preparation"
Fishbowl	See "To Encourage Active Listening"
Focused listing	Students brainstorm a list of ideas, solutions, examples, and so on.
Thinking time	You have students write down their ideas or reflect for 10 to 15 seconds before responding to a prompt.
Group summarizer	Assign an active listener in each small group to summarize others' ideas back to the group.
Comment summarizing	See "To Encourage Active Listening"
Prepared answers to discussion question	See "To Motivate Preparation"
Concrete deliverables	Students formulate a specific number of concrete deliverables (e.g., three examples) in 1 to 3 minutes. In small groups, they then discuss and select three examples to report to the class. This works well in large-class polls.
Snowball (with brainstorming)	You and your students toss a crumpled piece of paper around the room. The student who catches it or is closest to where it falls must respond to the brainstorming prompt.

Discussion Activity	Description
Round robin (with brainstorming)	You go around the room from student to student or group to group to solicit one new response to a brainstorming prompt. You should record each response where the whole class can see it.
Rotating facilitator	Near the end of the discussion, you ask a student to lead a discussion of "What haven't we said yet?"
Chalk talks	Students brainstorm in groups at the whiteboard.
Stand where you stand	Students stand in a corner of the room that represents their position on an issue. If each corner represents a different theoretical or analytical lens, students discuss an idea through the lens to which they are physically closest.
Folding line	Students arrange themselves along a line symbolizing a continuum of positions on a question or controversy. When the line "folds," those on one extreme make up a group with those on the other extreme, and they discuss or debate the issue. Or students can argue the other side's perspective and/or the extreme groups can try to persuade the "middle" group.
Role-play or simulation with debriefing	Some or all students participate in a role-play or simulation (the rest observe) and discuss their answers to debriefing questions.
Jigsaw	Students discuss a specialized topic in small groups of budding "experts" and then move into new groups, each with one representative of each of the expert groups, to teach their specialty.
Graphics	Students draw graphics (e.g., concept map, flowchart, matrix, concept circle diagram) to explain and discuss their organization of a body of knowledge.
Novel or outside-of-class stimuli	Students search for outside information or write about a personal experience related to the course material. They share and discuss their information or reflections in class.
Pinch points	In pairs or small groups, students discuss especially challenging new concepts ("pinch points") during lecture breaks—particularly their understanding of the concepts and the place of these concepts in the lecture organization.

Discussion Activity	*Description*
Students reactions to others' contributions	Students give their reactions, appraisals, extensions, qualifications, paraphrases, and the like to other students' contributions while you, as discussion moderator/facilitator, resist commenting.
Anonymous contributions	Students anonymously register or post their responses to private, sensitive, or controversial questions using sticky notes, anonymously submitted written answers, web- or app-based polling tools, or anonymous discussion boards or chat rooms. Anonymity encourages honesty and reduces anxiety.
Card-swapping, snowball-tossing	Students anonymously write a question or response on a 3x5-inch card and continuously swap cards for about 30 seconds to ensure that no one knows the origin of a given card. Alternatively, students use a piece of paper, crumple it up, toss it across the room, and retrieve someone else's crumpled paper. Students then share the question or comment on their new card or "snowball" in the discussion.
Three-penny rule	Give talkative students three pennies. They have to turn in a penny for each comment they make and can no longer comment when out of pennies.
Three-student rule	A student who contributes cannot speak again until at least three other students have contributed.
Opening activities	• Students summarize the last class. • Students explain the purpose of an event that happened during the last class, such as a demonstration, role-play, video, or debate. • Students answer easy recall questions on the assigned readings or other homework. • Students describe how they reacted emotionally to the assigned readings or other homework. • Students write a response to a substantive or reflective question on the assigned readings or other homework. • Students brainstorm what they already know about a topic or what outcomes they expect of an experiment or a situation.

Discussion Activity	Description
Stimulation activities	• One or more students read key text passages aloud and explain why these passages are important. • Students argue against a controversial question or position that you state. • Students reflect on and write their reaction to a provocative statement. • Students form small groups to answer questions. • Students engage in conversation before responding.
Participation money	You judge the value (in monetary terms) of a given comment and explain why, teaching students what constitutes high- and low-quality contributions.
Real participation money	You start the course by paying students a quarter for every good-faith contribution. After a few classes, you reward only the first contribution of the day, then only the higher-quality comments. Finally, you eliminate the quarters and reserve a $10 bill for an outstanding contribution.
Directing questions	You direct some questions to individual students or sectors of the room that have been quiet.
Private encouragement and rehearsal	Invite quiet students into your office hours and encourage them to participate. Give them a discussion prompt you'd like them to respond to during the next class and have them rehearse their answer with you.
Online extension	Extend classroom discussion to an online forum.
Discussion ground rules	You and/or your students set expectations for interactions early in the course, especially for discussing sensitive subjects that may arise. You may do this verbally or in your syllabus or written grading criteria or involve students in collaboratively developing ground rules or a course contract.
Explicit instructions for asynchronous online discussion	You choose topics or questions that closely connect with learning outcomes, give clear directions for posts (e.g., integrate with the readings), assess contributions against well-defined criteria, and set ground rules for interaction. You can also assign rotating "starter" and "wrapper" roles, ask students to generate prompts or test questions, and gently keep the discussion on track.

Discussion Activity	*Description*
Participation log	At the beginning of the course, inform your students that they will be recording and evaluating their contributions. On a form you distribute, students report specifically what and when they contributed to class and how their contribution advanced learning. Request two self-assessments during the course in which students identify their strengths and ways to improve both the quantity and quality of their participation.
Participation portfolio	At the beginning of the course, inform your students that they will be recording and evaluating their contributions using a participation rubric you have developed or adopted. Every 2 to 4 weeks, students submit in writing two, three, or four examples, your choice, of their best contributions or replies and give them a collective grade, which you can then accept, raise, or lower.
Deliberative dialogue	See "To Motivate Preparation"
Synchronous discussions via chat and webcam	You give students a participation grading rubric that you use to provide abundant feedback and encouragement. They also identify key takeaways in a class poll.
Collaborative autoethnography	Students follow a six-stage process focused around their own reflective prompts, acting as researchers using their personal stories as data to analyze in a broader social and relational context.
Mindful and contemplative informal writing	Students write a response to a complex prompt during the first 7 to 10 minutes of every class.
Chat and write	Students chat with others and write their responses before contributing publicly.
Research-centered labs	Students use lab sessions to conduct and discuss their authentic research.
Project-centered online discussions	Students use the online discussion forum to discuss their own field or research projects.

Note. Adapted from Herman, J. H., & Nilson, L. B. (2018). *Creating engaging discussions: Strategies for "avoiding crickets" in any size classroom and online* (pp. x–xv). Stylus.

REFERENCES

Abrami, P. C., Bernard, R. M., Borokhovski, E., Waddington, D. I., Wade, C. A., & Persson, T. (2014). Strategies for teaching students to think critically: A meta-analysis. *Review of Educational Research, 85*(2), 275–314. https://doi.org/10.3102/0034654314551063

Abrami, P. C., Bernard, R. M., Borokhovski, E., Wade, A., Surkes, M. A., Tamim, R., & Zhang, D. (2008). Instructional interventions affecting critical thinking skills and dispositions: A stage 1 meta-analysis. *Review of Educational Research, 78*(4), 1102–1134. https://doi.org/10.3102/0034654308326084

Achacoso, M. V. (2004). Post-test analysis: A tool for developing students' metacognitive awareness and self-regulation. In M. V. Achacoso & M. D. Svinivki, (Eds.), *Alternative strategies for evaluating student learning* (New Directions for Teaching and Learning, no. 100, pp. 115–119). Jossey Bass.

Alexander, B. (2020, May 11). How the coronavirus will change faculty life forever. *Chronicle of Higher Education.* https://www.chronicle.com/article/How-the-Coronavirus-Will/248750/

Alwill, M. (2018, April 11). Truth, belief, and critical thinking: A primer. *Medium.* https://medium.com/@michael.alwill/truth-belief-and-critical-thinking-a-primer-570fe80b26ee

Ambrose, S. A., Bridges, M. W., DiPietro, M., Lovett, M. C., & Norman, M. K. (2010). *How learning works: Seven research-based principles for smart teaching.* Jossey-Bass.

American Association of Colleges & Universities. (2009). *Critical thinking VALUE rubric.* http://www.aacu.org/value/rubrics/critical-thinking

American Psychiatric Association. (2019). *What are personality disorders?* https://www.psychiatry.org/patients-families/personality-disorders/what-are-personality-disorders

Anderson, L. W., & Krathwohl, D. R., with Airasian, P. W., Mayer, R. W., Pintrich, P. R., Raths, J., & Wittrock, M. C. (2000). *A taxonomy for learning, teaching, and assessing: A revision of Bloom's taxonomy of educational objectives.* Longman.

AP Fact Check. (n.d.). https://www.apnews.com/APFactCheck

Arum, R., Kim, J., Cho, E., & Roksa, J. (2012). *Documenting uncertain times: Postgraduate transitions of the academically adrift cohort.* Social Science Research Council. https://www.issuelab.org/resource/documenting-uncertain-times-postgraduate-transitions-of-the-academically-adrift-cohort.html

Arum, R., & Roksa, J. (2011). *Academically adrift: Limited learning on college campuses.* University of Chicago Press.

Atwood, M. (1985). *The handmaid's tale.* McClelland & Stewart.

Barkley, E. F. (2009). *Student engagement techniques: A handbook for college faculty.* Jossey-Bass.

Baxter, G., & Bowers, J. (1985). Beyond self-actualization: The persuasion of Pygmalion. *Training & Development Journal, 39*(8), 69–71.

Baxter Magolda, M. B. (1992). *Knowing and reasoning in college: Gender-related patterns in students' intellectual development.* Jossey-Bass.

Bean, J. C. (1996). *Engaging ideas: The professor's guide to integrating writing, critical thinking and active learning in the classroom.* Jossey-Bass.

Bloom, B., & Associates. (1956). *Taxonomy of educational objectives.* David McKay.

Bonwell, C. C. (2012). A disciplinary approach for teaching critical thinking. *National Teaching & Learning Forum, 21*(2), 1–7.

Bradbury, R. (1953). *Fahrenheit 451.* Ballantine Books.

Braun, N. M. (2004). Critical thinking in the business curriculum. *Journal of Education for Business, 79*(4), 232–236. https://doi.org/10.1080/08832323.2020.12088718

Brons, L. L. (n.d.) *Truth, rhetoric, and critical thinking.* http://www.lajosbrons.net/wp/criticalthinking.pdf

Brookes, D. T., & Lin, Y. (2010). Structuring classroom discourse using formative assessment rubrics. *Proceedings of the 2010 Physics Education Research Conference, 1289(5).* https://doi.org/10.1063/1.3515248

Brookfield, S. D. (2012a). *Developing critical thinkers.* https://static1.squarespace.com/static/5738a0ccd51cd47f81977fe8/t/5750ef2d62cd947608165cf2/1464921912225/Developing_Critical_Thinkers.pdf

Brookfield, S. D. (2012b). *Teaching for critical thinking: Tools and techniques to help students question their assumptions.* Jossey-Bass.

Brookfield, S. D., & Preskill, S. (2005). *Discussion as a way of teaching: Tools and techniques for democratic classrooms* (2nd ed.). Jossey-Bass.

Brookfield, S. D., & Preskill, S. (2016). *The discussion book: 50 great ways to get people talking.* Jossey-Bass.

Brown, P. (2014). *Red rising.* Del Rey Books.

Browne, M. N., & Keeley, S. M. (2018). *Asking the right questions: A guide to critical thinking* (12th ed.). Pearson.

Burbach, M., Matkin, G., & Fritz, S. (2004). Teaching critical thinking in an introductory leadership course utilizing active learning strategies: A confirmatory study. *College Student Journal, 38*(3), 482–493.

Burton, R. A. (2019, August 8). Our brains tell stories so we can live. *Nautilus.* http://nautil.us/issue/75/story/our-brains-tell-stories-so-we-can-live

Butler, H. A. (2017, October 3). Why do smart people do foolish things? Intelligence is not the same as critical thinking and the difference matters. *Scientific American.* https://www.scientificamerican.com/article/why-do-smart-people-do-foolish-things/

Casner-Lotto J., & Barrington, L. (2006). *Are they really ready to work? Employers' perspectives on the basic knowledge and applied skills of new entrants to the 21st century United States workforce.* The Conference Board. http://www.21stcenturyskills.org/documents/FINAL_REPORT_PDF09-29-06.pdf

Ceynar, T. (n.d.). *25 of the best family movies for teaching honesty, grit, courage & more.* A Fine Parent. https://afineparent.com/building-character/best-family-movies.html

Chozick, A. (2016, September 10). Hillary Clinton calls many Trump backers "deplorables," and G.O.P. pounces. *New York Times.* https://www.nytimes.com/2016/09/11/us/politics/hillary-clinton-basket-of-deplorables.htm

Coffield, F., with Costa, C., Müller, W., & Webber, J. (2014). *Beyond bulimic learning: Improving teaching in further education.* Institute of Education Press.

Collins, S. (2008). *The hunger games.* Scholastic.

Crenshaw, D. (2008). *The myth of multitasking: How "doing it all" gets nothing done.* Jossey-Bass.

Critical Thinking Community. (n.d.). *Welcome to the Center for Critical Thinking Community.* https://community.criticalthinking.org/

Davis, J. R., & Arend, B. D. (2013). *Facilitating seven ways of learning: A resource for more purposeful, effective, and enjoyable college teaching.* Stylus.

DiCaprio, L., Scorsese, M., Aziz, R., Tillinger, E., & McFarland, J. (Producers) & Scorsese, M. (Director). (2013). *The wolf of wall street* [Motion picture]. United States: Paramount.

Doyle, A. (2019, June 18). The top skills employers seek in college graduates. *The Balance.* https://www.thebalance.com/top-skills-employers-seek-in-college-grads-4030755

Dweck, C. S. (2007). *Mindset: The new psychology of success.* Random House.

Edwards, L. C. (2017). The craft of infusing critical thinking skills: A mixed-methods research on implementation and student outcome. *Journal on Centers for Teaching and Learning, 9,* 47–72. http://openjournal.lib.miamioh.edu/index.php/jctl/article/view/189

Elder, L., & Paul, R. (2006). Critical thinking and the art of substantive writing, Part II. *Journal of Developmental Education 29*(3), 38–39.

Elder, L., & Paul, R. (2007). *The thinker's guide to analytical thinking.* Foundation for Critical Thinking. https://www.criticalthinking.org/files/SAM_Analytic_Think2007b.pdf

Elder, L., & Paul, R. (2010). *Critical thinking development: A stage theory.* https://community.criticalthinking.org/viewDocument.php?doc=../content/library_for_educators/11/CriticalThinkingDevelopment.pdf&page=1

Elon University. (2019). *Elon poll report.* https://www.elon.edu/u/elon-poll/wp-content/uploads/sites/819/2019/07/2019_7_31-ElonPoll_Report.pdf

Etkina, E., Van Heuvelen, A., White-Brahmia, S., Brookes, D. T., Gentile, M., Murthy, S., Rosengrant, D., & Warren, A. (2006). Scientific abilities and their assessment. *Physical Review Special Topics: Physics Education Research, 2.* https://doi.org/10.1103/PhysRevSTPER.2.020103

Facione, P. A. (2011). *Think critically.* Prentice Hall.

Facione, P. A. (2020). *Critical thinking: What it is and why it counts.* http://www.insightassessment.com/pdsf_files/what&why2006.pdf

Facione, P. A., & Facione, N. C. (2007). Talking critical thinking. *Change: The Magazine of Higher Education, 39*(March–April), 38–44.

Facione, P. A., Facione, N. C., & Giancarlo, C. (2000). The disposition toward critical thinking: Its character, measurement, and relationship to critical thinking skills. *Journal of Informal Logic, 20*(1), 61–84. https://doi.org/10.22329/il.v20i1.2254

Facione, P. A., Facione, N. C., & Measured Reasons, LLC. (2011). *The holistic critical thinking scoring rubric—HCTSR: A tool for developing and evaluating critical thinking.* California Academic Press/Insight Assessment. http://www.deanza.edu/slo/icctaskforce/sample_rubric_gittens.pdf

FactCheck. (n.d.). https://www.factcheck.org/

Farrington, R. (2020, February 11). The top investment scams costing investors millions. *The College Investor.* https://thecollegeinvestor.com/1944/top-investment-scams/

Fink, L. D. (2013). *Creating significant learning experiences: An integrated approach to designing college courses* (2nd ed.). Jossey-Bass.

FlackCheck. (n.d.). https://www.flackcheck.org/

Flaherty, C. (2017, February 3). AAC&U releases report on national, large-scale look at student learning. *Inside Higher Ed.* https://www.insidehighered.com/news/2017/02/23/aacu-releases-report-national-large-scale-look-student-learning

Foner, E. (2010). *The fiery trial: Abraham Lincoln and American slavery.* W. W. Norton & Company.

Foundation for Critical Thinking (2019a). *Socratic questioning.* https://community.criticalthinking.org/viewDocument.php?doc=../content/library_for_educators/193/Chapter20-SocraticQuestioning.pdf&page=1

Foundation for Critical Thinking (2019b). *The role of Socratic questioning in thinking.* https://community.criticalthinking.org/viewDocument.php?doc=../content/library_for_educators/22/TheRoleofSocraticQuestioninginThinking.pdf&page=1

Foundation for Critical Thinking. (n.d.). Library for educators. *Critical Thinking Community.* https://community.criticalthinking.org/libraryForEducators.php

Friedman, W. J. (2019). *Critical thinking is not critical, just looking for truth & reality: The heart of asking questions that reveal "what is."* MentalHelp. https://www.mentalhelp.net/blogs/critical-thinking-is-not-critical-just-looking-for-truth-amp-reality-the-heart-of-asking-questions-that-reveal-quot-what-is-quot/

Goldman, E. (n.d.). The 5 biggest investment scams in history. *Alternative Investment Coach.* http://alternativeinvestmentcoach.com/biggest-investment-scams/

Gore, D. (2019, August 21). *Kudlow's unsupported USMCA jobs claim.* FactCheck. https://www.factcheck.org/2019/08/kudlows-unsupported-usmca-jobs-claim/

Grossmann, I., Dorfman, A., Oakes, H., Santos, H., Vohs, K. D., & Scholer, A. (2019, May 8). Training for wisdom: The illeist diary method. *PsyArXiv.* https://doi.org/10.31234/osf.io/a5fgu

Hall, M. (2013). *Perry's scheme—Understanding the intellectual development of college-age students.* The Innovative Instructor Blog. https://ii.library.jhu.edu/2013/12/13/perrys-scheme-understanding-the-intellectual-development-of-college-age-students/

Halpern, D. F. (1999, Winter). Teaching for critical thinking: Helping college students develop the skills and dispositions of a critical thinker. (New Directions for Teaching and Learning, no, 80, 69–74). Wiley. https://doi.org/10.1002/tl.8005

Halpern, D. F. (2014). *Thought and knowledge: An introduction to critical thinking* (5th ed.). Psychology Press. https://archive.org/details/Thought_and_Knowledge_An_Introduction_to_Critical_Thinking_by_Diane_F._Halpern/page/n15

Halvorson, H. G. (2014). The key to great feedback? Praise the process, not the person. *99U.* http://99u.com/articles/19442/the-key-to-great-feedback-praise-the-process-not-the-person

Herman, J. H., & Nilson, L. B. (2018). *Creating engaging discussions: Strategies for "avoiding crickets" in any size classroom and online.* Stylus.

Hesse, H. (1951). *Siddhartha* (H. Rosner, Trans.). New Directions Publishing. (Original work published 1922)

Hong, P. Y. (2004, January 26). Money top goal of college freshmen. *Los Angeles Times.* http://articles.latimes.com/2004/jan/26/local/me-survey26

Howard, J. R. (2015). *Discussion in the college classroom: Getting your students engaged and participating in person and online.* Jossey-Bass.

Huber, C. R., & Kuncel, N. R. (2016). Does college teach critical thinking? A meta-analysis. *Review of Educational Research, 86*(2), 431–468. https//:doi.org/10.3102/0034654315605917

Huxley, A. (1932). *Brave new world.* Chatto & Windus.

Insight Assessment. (2013a). *California Critical Thinking Skills Tests scales, description.* http://www.insightassessment.com/Products/Products-Summary/Critical-Thinking-Skills-Tests/California-Critical-Thinking-Skills-Test-Numeracy-CCTST-Nl

Insight Assessment. (2013b). *Sample items from the California Critical Thinking Skills Test (CCTST).* https://www.insightassessment.com/Resources/Teaching-Training-and-Learning-Tools/node_1487

Insight Assessment. (2019). *Evaluating written argumentation rubric.* https://www.insightassessment.com/var/ezflow_site/storage/pdf/Evaluating+Written+Argumentation+-+REWA.pdf

Insight Assessment. (2020). *Advancing thinking worldwide.* https://www.insightassessment.com/Resources/

Intentional Insights. (2017). *Intentional Insights: Live better. Think better.* https://intentionalinsights.org/

Investopedia. (2020, June 3). *How does a pump and dump scam work?* https://www.investopedia.com/ask/answers/05/061205.asp

Jenkins, R. (2017, February 2). What is critical thinking anyway? *Chronicle Vitae.* https://chroniclevitae.com/news/1691-what-is-critical-thinking-anyway

Johnson, D. W., Johnson, R. T., & Smith, K. A. (1991). *Active learning: Cooperation in the college classroom.* Interaction Books.

Junco, R., & Cotton, S. R. (2012). No A 4 U: The relationship between multitasking and academic performance. *Computers and Education, 59*(2), 505–514. http://www.sciencedirect.com/science/article/pii/S036013151100340X

Kraus, S., Sears, S. R., & Burke, B. L. (2013). Is truthiness enough? Classroom activities for encouraging evidence-based critical thinking. *Journal of Effective Teaching, 13*(2), 83–93. https://gato-docs.its.txstate.edu/jcr:450ce4f6-477c-466a-983d-c846afcf1755/EvidenceAnalysisModule.pdf

Kuh, G. D. (2019, October 9). Why skills training can't replace higher education. *Harvard Business Review.* https://hbr.org/2019/10/why-skills-training-cant-replace-higher-education?

Lepp, A., Barkley, J. E., & Karpinski, A. C. (2014). The relationship between cell phone use, academic performance, anxiety, and satisfaction with life in college students. *Computers in Human Behavior, 31,* 343–350. http://www.sciencedirect.com/science/article/pii/S0747563213003993#

Lockhead, J., & Whimbey, A. (1987). Teaching analytical reasoning through thinking aloud pair problem-solving. In J. E. Stice (Ed.), *Developing critical thinking and problem-solving abilities* (New Directions for Teaching and Learning, no. 30, pp. 73–92). Jossey-Bass. https://doi.org/10.1002/tl.37219873007

Lowry, L. (1993). *The Giver.* Houghton Mifflin.

Maslow, A. H. (1954). *Motivation and personality.* Harper.

Massa, L. J., & Kasimatis, M. (2017). *Meaningful and manageable program assessment: A how-to guide for higher education faculty.* Stylus.

McConnell, K. D., & Rhodes, T. L. (2017). *On solid ground: VALUE report 2017.* AAC&U. https://www.aacu.org/OnSolidGroundVALUE

McDaniel, M. A., Howard, D. C., & Einstein, G. O. (2009). The Read-Recite-Review study strategy: Effective and portable. *Psychological Science, 20*(4), 516–522. https://doi.org/10.1111/j.1467-9280.2009.02325.x

McDonald, J. (2019, August 20). *Williamson misleads on children's health, vaccines.* FactCheck. https://www.factcheck.org/2019/08/williamson-misleads-on-childrens-health-vaccines/

Media Bias/Fact Check (n.d.). https://mediabiasfactcheck.com/

Mohdin, A., & van der Zee, B. (2018, December 5). Killed for speaking the truth: Tribute to 9 journalists murdered in 2018. *The Guardian.* https://www.theguardian.com/media/2018/dec/05/journalists-murdered-khashoggi-kuciak-panama-papers

Moore, W. S. (2001). *The Perry network: Overview of Perry Scheme.* The Perry Network. http://perrynetwork.org/?page_id=2

Murphy, D., Campbell, C., & Garavan, T. (1999). The Pygmalion effect reconsidered: Its implications for education, training and workplace learning. *Journal of European Industrial Training, 23*(4/5), 238–251. https://doi.org/10.1108/03090599910272112

NACE Staff. (2018, December 12). *Employers want to see these attributes on students' résumés.* National Association of Colleges and Employers. https://www.naceweb.org/talent-acquisition/candidate-selection/employers-want-to-see-these-attributes-on-students-resumes/

Nelson, C. E. (1993, November 19). *Fostering critical thinking and mature valuing across the curriculum.* Workshop presented at the 13th Annual Lilly Conference on College Teaching, Oxford, OH.

Nelson, C. E. (2000). How can students who are reasonably bright and who are trying hard to do the work still flunk? *National Teaching and Learning Forum, 9*(5), 7–8.

Nichols, H. (2017, October 16). What does caffeine do to your body? *MedicalNews-Today.* https://www.medicalnewstoday.com/articles/285194#takeaway

Nilson, L. B. (1997). Critical thinking as an exercise in courage. *National Teaching and Learning Forum, (6)*2, 1–4.

Nilson, L. B. (2013). *Creating self-regulated learners: Strategies to strengthen students' self-awareness and learning skills.* Stylus.

Nilson, L. B. (2015). *Specifications grading: Restoring rigor, motivating students, and saving faculty time.* Stylus.

Nilson, L. B. (2016a). *Infusing critical thinking into your courses.* Magna Publications. https://www.magnapubs.com/product/online-courses/infusing-critical-thinking-into-your-courses-2/

Nilson, L. B. (2016b). *Teaching at its best: A research-based resource for college instructors* (4th ed.). Jossey-Bass.

Nisbett, R. E. (1993). *Rules for reasoning.* Lawrence Erlbaum.

Northeastern Illinois University. (2006). *General education critical thinking rubric.* https://cft.vanderbilt.edu/wp-content/uploads/sites/59/Rubric-Critical-Thinking-NE-Illinois.pdf

Nosich, G. M. (2012). *Learning to think things through: A guide to critical thinking across the curriculum* (4th ed.). Pearson/Prentice Hall.

Nuhfer, E., Harrington, R., Pasztor, S., & Whorf, S. (2014). Metadisciplinary awareness can illuminate the meaning, quality, and integrity of college degrees: Educating in fractal patterns XL. *National Teaching and Learning Forum, 23*(4), 9–11.

Nussbaum, M. (1997). *Poetic justice: The literary imagination and public life.* Beacon Press.

Oljar, E., & Koukal, D. R. (2019, February 3). How to make students better thinkers. *Chronicle of Higher Education.* https://www.chronicle.com/article/How-to-Make-Students-Better/245576

OpenSecrets. (n.d.). https://www.opensecrets.org/

Orlando, L., & Silvio, A. (2017, September 14). *60 Minutes.* [Television broadcast]. CBS News.

Orwell, G. (1945). *Animal farm.* Secker & Warburg.

Orwell, G. (1949). *Nineteen eighty-four.* Secker & Warburg.

Osborne, J. F. (2010). An argument for arguments in science classes. *R&D, 91*(4), 62–65. https://doi.org/10.1177/003172171009100413

Paris, B. (2016, November 29). Roadblocks to better critical-thinking skills are embedded in the college experience (essay). *Inside Higher Ed.* https://www.insidehighered.com/views/2016/11/29/roadblocks-better-critical-thinking-skills-are-embedded-college-experience-essay

Parkes, J., & Zimmaro, D. (2016). *Learning and assessing with multiple-choice questions in college classrooms.* Routledge.

Patrone, P. (2019, January 1). The skills companies needs most in 2019. *LinkedIn.* https://learning.linkedin.com/blog/top-skills/the-skills-companies-need-most-in-2019--and-how-to-learn-them

Paul, R. (2004). *The state of critical thinking today.* http://www.criticalthinking.org/pages/the-state-of-critical-thinking-today/523

Paul, R., & Elder, L. (2014). *Critical thinking: Concepts & tools* (7th ed.). Foundation for Critical Thinking.

Paul, R., Elder, L., & Bartell, T. (2013). *Study of 38 public universities and 28 private universities to determine faculty emphasis on critical thinking in instruction.* https://www.criticalthinking.org/pages/study-of-38-public-universities-and-28-private-universities-to-determine-faculty-emphasis-on-critical-thinking-in-instruction/598

Payette, P., & Barnes, B. (2017). Combatting the "truthiness" tendencies. *National Teaching and Learning Forum, 26*(4), 7–9.

Pedersen, A. T., & Ottesen, B. (2003). Issues to debate on the Women's Health Initiative (WHI) study. Epidemiology or randomized clinical trials—time out for hormone replacement therapy studies? *Human Reproduction, 18*(11), 2241–2244. https://doi.org/10.1093/humrep/deg435

Perry, W. G. (1968). *Forms of intellectual and ethical development in the college years: A scheme.* Holt, Rinehart & Winston.

PolitiFact. (n.d.). https://www.politifact.com/

Pro-Truth Pledge, The. (n.d.). *The pro-truth pledge.* https://www.protruthpledge.org

Ramsey, L. (2019, April 11). The rise and fall of Theranos, the blood-testing startup that went from Silicon Valley darling to facing fraud charges. *Business Insider.* https://www.businessinsider.com/the-history-of-silicon-valley-unicorn-theranos-and-ceo-elizabeth-holmes-2018-5

Rappaport, W. J. (2003). *William Perry's scheme of intellectual and ethical development.* State University of New York at Buffalo. https://cse.buffalo.edu/~rapaport/perry.positions.html

Reecekesson. (2019). *20 inspirational movies with important life lessons.* https://www.imdb.com/list/ls070596678/

Robinson, D. H., Katayama, A. D., DuBois, N. E., & Devaney, T. (1998). Interactive effects of graphic organizers and delayed review of concept application. *Journal of Experimental Education, 67*(1), 17–31. https://doi.org/10.1080/00220979809598342

Robinson, D. H., & Kiewra, K. A. (1995). Visual argument: Graphic organizers are superior to outlines in improving learning from text. *Journal of Educational Psychology, 87*(3), 455–467. https://doi.org/10.1037/0022-0663.87.3.455

Rosenthal, R., & Jacobson, L. (1968). *Pygmalion in the classroom: Teacher expectation and pupils' intellectual development.* Holt, Rinehart & Winston.

Roth, M. S. (2010, January 3). Beyond critical thinking. *Chronicle of Higher Education.* http://chronicle.com/article/Beyond-Critical-Thinking/63288/

Rutgers Physics and Astronomy Education Research. (2014). *Rubrics.* Scientific Abilities. https://sites.google.com/site/scientificabilities/rubrics

Schlueter, J. (2016, June 7). Can colleges truly teach critical thinking skills? *Inside Higher Ed.* https://www.insidehighered.com/views/2016/06/07/can-colleges-truly-teach-critical-thinking-skills-essay

Schwartz, B. (2015, June 18). What "learning how to think" really means. *Chronicle of Higher Education.* https://www.chronicle.com/article/What-Learning-How-to-Think/230965

Schwartz, B., & Sharpe, K. (2011). *Practical wisdom: The right way to do the right thing.* Penguin Group.

Seesholtz, M., & Polk, B. (2009, October 10). Two professors, one valuable lesson: How to respectfully disagree. *Chronicle of Higher Education.* http://chronicle.com/article/Two-Professors-One-Valuable/48901/

Self-Regulated Learning Program, The. (n.d.). *Home page.* http://www.selfregulatedlearning.blogspot.com/

Sibley, J. (2014). *Writing better multiple-choice questions: How effective are your multiple-choice questions?* Magna Publications Online Seminar. https://www.magnapubs.com/online-seminars/writing-better-multiple-choice-questions-11972-1.html

Silberman, M. (1996). *Active learning: 101 strategies to teach any subject.* Pearson.

Skills You Need. (2019). *Critical thinking.* https://www.skillsyouneed.com/learn/critical-thinking.html

Smith, A. (2013, December 11). Five things you didn't know about Bernie Madoff's epic scam. *CNN Business.* https://money.cnn.com/2013/12/10/news/companies/bernard-madoff-ponzi/

Snopes. (n.d.). https://www.snopes.com/fact-check/

Snowden, E. (2019). *Permanent record.* Metropolitan Books.

Stephenson, N. (1992). *Snow crash.* Bantam Books.

Stolzenberg, E. B., Eagan, M. K., Aragon, M. C., Cesar-Davis, N. M., Jacobo, S., Couch, V., Rios-Aguilar, C. (2018). *The American freshman: National norms fall 2017.* Higher Education Research Institute, UCLA. https://www.heri.ucla.edu/monographs/TheAmericanFreshman2017.pdf

Strauss, K. (2016, May 17). These are the skills bosses say new college grads do not have. *Forbes.* https://www.forbes.com/sites/karstenstrauss/2016/05/17/these-are-the-skills-bosses-say-new-college-grads-do-not-have/#5181a7d45491

Tartakovsky, M. (2018, July 8). Why ruminating is unhealthy and how to stop. *PsychCentral.* https://psychcentral.com/blog/why-ruminating-is-unhealthy-and-how-to stop/

Taylor, S. M. (2010, September 21). Writing comments that lead to learning. *Faculty Focus.* https://www.facultyfocus.com/articles/effective-teaching-strategies/writing-comments-that-lead-to-learning/

Tremblay, K. R. Jr., & Downey, E. P. (2004). Identifying and evaluating research-based publications: Enhancing undergraduate student critical thinking skills. *Education, 124*(4), 734–740.

Truth or Fiction (n.d.). https://www.truthorfiction.com/

Tsipursky, G., & Ward, T. (2020). *Pro truth: A practical plan for putting truth back into politics.* Changemaker Books.

University of Minnesota. (2012). *Online archive of context-rich problems: Linear Kinematics: Two-dimensional motion at a constant acceleration (projectile).* Physics

Education Research and Development Group. https://groups.spa.umn.edu/phy-sed/Research/CRP/on-lineArchive/ola.html

U.S. Census Bureau. (2019). *Survey of income and program participation, 2014 panel, wave 4.* https://www.census.gov/programs-surveys/sipp/data/datasets/2014-panel/wave-4.html

van Gelder, T. (2005). Teaching critical thinking: Some lessons from cognitive science. *College Teaching, 53*(1), 41–46.

Van Noorden, R. (2011). Science publishing: The trouble with retractions. *Nature, 478,* 26–28. https://doi.org/10.1038/478026a

Vekiri, I. (2002). What is the value of graphical displays in learning? *Educational Psychology Review, 14*(3), 261–312. https://doi.org/10.1023/A:1016064429161

Vick, K. (2019). The guardians and the war on truth. *Time.* https://time.com/per son-of-the-year-2018-the-guardians/

Visible Learning. (2017). Backup of Hattie's ranking list of 256 influences and effect sizes related to student achievement [table view]. https://visible-learning.org/backup-hattie-ranking-256-effects-2017/

Wang, Y., & Lin, L. (2014). Pygmalion effect on junior English teaching. *Advances in Language and Literacy Studies, 5*(4), 18–23. https://doi.org/10.7575/aiac .alls.v.5n.6p.l8

Washington State University. (2009). *Critical and integrative thinking rubric.* https://www.colorado.edu/sei/sites/default/files/attached-files/wsu-critical-thinking-rubric-2009.pdf

Wiggins, G., & McTighe, J. (2005). *Understanding by design.* Association for Super-vision and Curriculum Development.

Williamson, O. M. (2018). *Master list of logical fallacies.* http://utminers.utep.edu/omwilliamson/ENGL1311/fallacies.htm

Willingham, D. T. (2007, Summer). Critical thinking: Why is it so hard to teach? *American Educator,* 8–19. http://www.aft.org//sites/default/files/periodicals/Crit_Thinking.pdf

Willingham, D. T. (2019, May). *How to teach critical thinking.* (Education: Future Frontiers Occasional Paper.) USW Department of Education, Australia. http://www.danielwillingham.com/uploads/5/0/0/7/5007325/willingham_2019_nsw_critical_thinking.pdf

Wolcott, S. L. (2006). *College faculty handbook: Steps for better thinking.* http://www .wolcottlynch.com/educator-resources.html

WolcottLynch. (n.d.). *Steps for better thinking.* www.wolcottlynch.com

Zimmerman, B. J., Moylan, A., Hudesman, J., White, N., & Flugman, B. (2011). Enhancing self-reflection and mathematics achievement of at-risk students at an urban technical college. *Psychological Test and Assessment Modeling, 53*(1), 141–160. https://www.gc.cuny.edu/CUNY_GC/media/CUNY-Graduate-Center/PDF/Centers/CASE/enhancing_self_reflection.pdf

ABOUT THE AUTHOR

Linda B. Nilson is founding director emeritus of the Office of Teaching Effectiveness and Innovation (OTEI) at Clemson University and author of *Teaching at Its Best: A Research-Based Resource for College Instructors*, now in its fourth edition (Jossey-Bass, 2016). She also wrote *The Graphic Syllabus and the Outcomes Map: Communicating Your Course* (Anker/Jossey-Bass, 2007), *Creating Self-Regulated Learners: Strategies to Strengthen Students' Self-Awareness and Learning Skills* (Stylus, 2013), and *Specifications Grading: Restoring Rigor, Motivating Students, and Saving Faculty Time* (Stylus, 2015). Her latest books are *Online Teaching at Its Best: Merging Instructional Design With Teaching and Learning Research* with Ludwika A. Goodson (Jossey-Bass/Wiley, 2018; 2nd edition forthcoming in 2021) and *Creating Engaging Discussions: Strategies for "Avoiding Crickets" in Any Size Classroom and Online* with Jennifer H. Herman (Stylus, 2018).

In addition, she also coedited *Enhancing Learning With Laptops in the Classroom* (Jossey-Bass, 2005) and Volumes 25 through 28 of *To Improve the Academy: Resources for Faculty, Instructional, and Organizational Development* (Anker, 2007, 2008; Jossey-Bass, 2009, 2010). *To Improve the Academy* is the major publication of the Professional and Organizational Development (POD) Network in Higher Education.

Nilson's career as a full-time faculty development director spanned over 25 years. In this time and since she retired from Clemson University in 2016, she has published many articles and book chapters and has given over 550 keynotes, webinars, and live workshops at conferences, colleges, and universities both nationally and internationally. She has spoken on dozens of topics related to course design, best teaching and assessment practices, scholarly productivity, and academic career matters. In her recent articles, she identifies the characteristics of a strong center for teaching and learning, ascertains key teaching effectiveness outcomes for faculty, raises serious questions about the validity of student ratings, and describes instructor-friendly ways to measure course-level learning that are suitable for the most rigorous faculty review.

Before coming to Clemson University, Nilson directed the teaching centers at Vanderbilt University and the University of California, Riverside, where she developed the "disciplinary cluster" approach to training teaching assistants out of a centralized unit. She has also taught graduate seminars on college teaching. She entered the area of educational/faculty development while she was on the sociology faculty at the University of California, Los Angeles. After distinguishing herself as an excellent instructor, her department selected her to set up and supervise its teaching assistant training program. In sociology, her research focused on occupations and work, social stratification, political sociology, and disaster behavior.

Nilson has held leadership positions in the POD Network, Toastmasters International, Mensa, and the Southern Regional Faculty and Instructional Development Consortium. She was a National Science Foundation Fellow at the University of Wisconsin, Madison, where she received her PhD and MS degrees in sociology. She completed her undergraduate work in 3 years at the University of California, Berkeley, where she was elected to Phi Beta Kappa.

She lives with her retired husband, Greg Bauernfeind, and their somewhat pampered miniature Schnauzer in Anderson, South Carolina.

Faculty Development books from Stylus Publishing

Advancing the Culture of Teaching on Campus
ow a Teaching Center Can Make a Difference
Edited by Constance Cook and Matthew Kaplan
Foreword by Lester P. Monts

Faculty Mentoring
A Practical Manual for Mentors, Mentees, Administrators,
and Faculty Developers
Susan L. Phillips and Susan T. Dennison
Foreword by Milton D. Cox

Faculty Retirement
Best Practices for Navigating the Transition
Edited by Claire Van Ummersen, Jean McLaughlin and
Lauren Duranleau
Foreword by Lotte Bailyn

The Prudent Professor
Planning and Saving for a Worry-Free Retirement from
Academe
Edwin M. Bridges and Brian D. Bridges

Teaching Across Cultural Strengths
A Guide to Balancing Integrated and Individuated Cultural
Frameworks in College Teaching
Alicia Fedelina Chávez and Susan Diana Longerbeam
Foreword by Joseph L. White

Why Students Resist Learning
A Practical Model for Understanding and Helping Students
Edited by Anton O. Tolman and Janine Kremling
Foreword by John Tagg

Student Development books from Stylus Publishing

Advancing Black Male Student Success From Preschool Through Ph.D.
Edited by Shaun R. Harper and J. Luke Wood

The New Science of Learning Edition 2
How to Learn in Harmony With Your Brain
Terry Doyle and Todd D. Zakrajsek
Foreword by Kathleen F. Gabriel

Advancing Online Teaching
Creating Equity-Based Digital Learning Environments
Kevin Kelly and Todd D. Zakrajsek
Foreword by Michelle Pacansky-Brock

Real-Time Student Assessment
Meeting the Imperative for Improved Time to Degree, Closing the Opportunity Gap, and Assuring Student Competencies for 21st-Century Needs
Peggy L. Maki
Foreword by George D. Kuh

Successful STEM Mentoring Initiatives for Underrepresented Students
A Research-Based Guide for Faculty and Administrators
Becky Wai-Ling Packard
Foreword by Norman L. Fortenberry

Teach Students How to Learn
Strategies You Can Incorporate Into Any Course to Improve Student Metacognition, Study Skills, and Motivation
Saundra Yancy McGuire
With Stephanie McGuire
Foreword by Thomas Angelo

Teaching and Learning books from Stylus

Learner-Centered Teaching
Putting the Research on Learning into Practice
Terry Doyle
Foreword by Todd D. Zakrajsek

Of Education, Fishbowls, and Rabbit Holes
Rethinking Teaching and Liberal Education for an Interconnected World
Jane Fried With Peter Troiano
Foreword by Dawn R. Person

Creating Wicked Students
Designing Courses for a Complex World
Paul Hanstedt

Dynamic Lecturing
Research-Based Strategies to Enhance Lecture Effectiveness
Christine Harrington and Todd Zakrajsek
Foreword by José Antonio Bowen

Designing a Motivational Syllabus
Creating a Learning Path for Student Engagement
Christine Harrington and Melissa Thomas
Foreword by Kathleen F. Gabriel

Course-Based Undergraduate Research
Educational Equity and High-Impact Practice
Edited by Nancy H. Hensel
Foreword by Cathy N. Davidson

Teaching and Technology books from Stylus

High-Impact Practices in Online Education
Research and Best Practices
Edited by Kathryn E. Linder and Chrysanthemum
Mattison Hayes
Foreword by Kelvin Thompson

Designing the Online Learning Experience
Evidence-Based Principles and Strategies
Simone C. O. Conceição and Les L. Howles
Foreword by B. Jean Mandernach

The Blended Course Design Workbook
A Practical Guide
Kathryn E. Linder

Clickers in the Classroom
Edited by David S. Goldstein and Peter D. Wallis
Foreword by James Rhem

Jump-Start Your Online Classroom
Mastering Five Challenges in Five Days
David S. Stein and Constance E. Wanstreet

Creating Self-Regulated Learners

*Strategies to Strengthen Students'
Self-Awareness and Learning Skills*

Linda B. Nilson

Foreword by Barry J. Zimmerman

"Linda B. Nilson has provided a veritable gold mine of effective learning strategies that are easy for faculty to teach and for students to learn. Most students can turn poor course performance into success if they are taught even a few of the strategies presented. However, relatively few students will implement new strategies if they are not required to do so by instructors. Nilson shows how to seamlessly introduce learning strategies into classes, thereby maximizing the possibility that students will become self-regulated learners who take responsibility for their own learning."—**Saundra McGuire**, *Assistant Vice Chancellor (Ret.) & Professor of Chemistry, Louisiana State University*

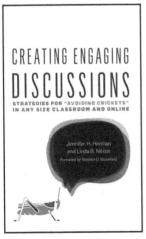

Creating Engaging Discussions

*Strategies for "Avoiding Crickets" in Any
Size Classroom and Online*

Jennifer H. Herman and
Linda B. Nilson

Foreword by Stephen D. Brookfield

"I've stolen a lot from this book. I regard myself as an avid collector of new pedagogic baubles and love it when I stumble across a new way to engage my students as I have done many times by reading Herman and Nilson's work. I have no doubt that as you read this book your own collection of discussion-based teaching strategies will be significantly enlarged."—**Stephen D. Brookfield**, *University of St. Thomas, Minneapolis-St. Paul*

Understanding How We Learn

Applying Key Educational Psychology Concepts in the Classroom

Todd D. Zakrajsek

This succinct, jargon-free, and user-friendly volume offers faculty an introduction to 35 concepts from educational psychology that illuminate what's going through the minds of learners as they grapple with new information.

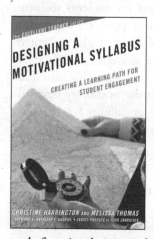

Designing a Motivational Syllabus

Creating a Learning Path for Student Engagement

Christine Harrington and Melissa Thomas

Foreword by Kathleen F. Gabriel

"Harrington and Thomas insightfully apply principles from the motivation research literature to demonstrate how course syllabi can be powerful tools for stimulating students' enthusiasm and motivation to actively engage in course activities. While the book is an invaluable resource for designing a syllabus that maps out a path for student success, it also provides information on course design, assessment, and teaching approaches. It is a must-read for all faculty who want to construct a syllabus that is sure to increase student engagement and learning!"—*Saundra McGuire*, *(Ret.) Assistant Vice Chancellor & Professor of Chemistry; Director Emerita, Center for Academic Success, Louisiana State University; Author of Teach Students How to Learn*

22883 Quicksilver Drive
Sterling, VA 20166-2019   Subscribe to our e-mail alerts: www.Styluspub.com